They Say The Lion

by the same author

THE PRIDE AND THE FALL: IRAN 1974–1979

They Say The Lion

Britain's Legacy to the Arabs: A Personal Memoir

Anthony Parsons

JONATHAN CAPE
THIRTY-TWO BEDFORD SQUARE LONDON

First published 1986
Copyright © 1986 by Anthony Parsons

Jonathan Cape Ltd, 32 Bedford Square, London WC1B 3EL

British Library Cataloguing in Publication Data

Parsons, Anthony, *1922*–
They say the lion.
1. Diplomacy—History—20th century 2. Arab
countries—Foreign relations
I. Title
327.2'0974927   DS63

ISBN 0-224-02829-4

Printed and bound in Great Britain
by Butler & Tanner Ltd, Frome and London

To my wife Sheila without whom I would never have had these experiences and who made even the most tedious moments enjoyable

Contents

Illustrations

Uncredited photographs are taken from the author's personal archives.

They say the Lion and the Lizard keep
The Courts where Jamshyd gloried and drank deep.

Edward Fitzgerald, *Omar Khayyam*

Introduction

Any student of British history knows that, from the late eighteenth century onwards, the relatively impecunious sons of Anglo-Irish families provided many of the vertebrae of the backbone of what George Orwell described as the Imperial middle class. My great-great-grandfather was part of this tradition. He left Ireland at the age of eighteen as an ensign in the Bengal Army of the East India Company and died in India over sixty years later, having never returned to Britain. My great-grandfather followed him into the Bengal Army about ten years before the Mutiny and also spent the rest of his active life in India, latterly in the Political Service. My grandfather, my father and virtually all my senior relations passed their lives in the service of the Empire. I am the last of my direct line to serve the state, first in the Army and then, for the greater part of my career, in the Diplomatic Service.

It is therefore no great wonder that, when I grew up in the 1920s and 1930s, I was only dimly aware that there were such things as careers outside government service for the likes of me: one of the first books which I remember reading was a large, blue-bound volume entitled *The Empire Story*. My childhood and adolescence, as was the case with all my contemporaries, were overcast by the shadow of the Great War behind us and the shadow of an inevitable second round with Germany before us. Europe was a place of storms and I think we took it for granted that we would sooner or later end up in a trench in Flanders. The only rock of certainty for myself and my colleagues at school, the majority of whom came from backgrounds identical to mine, was that the British Empire was eternal. Life without it was unimaginable. What indeed would we do with our lives, in the unlikely event of our surviving the trench in Flanders, if there was no India, no Africa in which to earn our living for twenty or thirty years before retiring to some appropriate part of the southern English countryside? Whether we served our apprenticeship at Sandhurst, Woolwich, Oxford or Cambridge, the ultimate destination would be 'overseas'; that is, some part of the imperial possessions.

Well, it did not work out exactly as we had anticipated. We were right about one thing. There was another war with Germany and all of us were caught up in it. The Flanders experience was not, however, repeated and more of my generation of young Englishmen survived than had in my father's day. In my case the chances of war took me first to the Middle East, then to Italy and, after the cessation of hostilities, to Palestine during the last three years of the British Mandate. These fortuitous peregrinations – I could equally easily have finished up in any other part of the world – prepared the way for my subsequent career as a Middle Eastern specialist in the British Diplomatic Service, a career which terminated with my retirement thirty-four years later to a house on the edge of Dartmoor – right again.

Chance is the arbiter of the lives of most of us. When in Palestine I had served with a para-military force composed almost entirely of Arabs. I had accordingly been obliged to learn Arabic. In early 1946 the War Office had offered me a choice – to be made at twenty-four hours' notice – of demobilisation or a regular commission. I chose the latter, more out of force of habit and upbringing than for any positive reason. Hence when I returned from Palestine in 1948 I found myself still in the Army. My wife and I were not attracted by the prospect of peacetime soldiering, and I fastened greedily on to an Army Council Instruction which permitted officers whose education had been interrupted by the war (I had been due to go up to Oxford in 1940 but had joined the Army instead) to be released from military duty for two years to complete their university education. I was granted an interview with a general at local Area Headquarters. He asked me what I intended to read at Oxford. 'English literature,' I answered unhesitatingly. There was an explosion. As the smoke cleared the general was saying that he had no intention of allowing me to waste the taxpayer's money (I was to be paid in my rank of Captain) swanning about reading Shakespeare and spouting poetry. Was there anything I could study which would be of use to the government? 'Well,' I replied with some reluctance, 'I do know Arabic.' The general, who seemed surprisingly sympathetic to my desire to escape from regimental duty, agreed to forward my application provided that I could find myself a place at a college and was accepted by the School of Oriental Studies. So it turned out. I often wonder how my life would have unfolded if he had agreed to my original request.

Where I and my school friends had been hopelessly off target in the 1930s was in our conviction of the permanence of the Empire. If someone had told us that, by the time we were in our forties, the great structure on which the sun never set would have disappeared, with the exception of a handful of rocks and islands, plus one or two disputed territories, we would have regarded him as a lunatic. Had he gone on to say that Britain would have become a medium-sized European power, economically poorer than France, in a world dominated by the United States and the Soviet Union, any last doubts about his sanity would have been removed.

As it turned out, I had my career in the service of the state, as my ancestors would have expected, but not in a form which they could easily have imagined. For well over thirty years, I was involved, in the Middle East, in London and at the United Nations in New York, in the process of decolonisation or, for the greater part of the time, in the long retreat from what used to be known as British spheres of influence.

Many excellent books have been written about the British Raj in India and about the direct colonial experience in other parts of the world. I have chosen a related theme based on personal experience. With the exception of Aden, the Middle East was never part of the British Empire. From Egypt to Persia, most of the countries in the region were the Asiatic provinces of the Ottoman Empire. But, from the beginning of the nineteenth century until the period im-

Introduction

mediately following the Second World War, British influence was predominant. Britain needed either to control these territories or to deny control of them to her rivals, in the interest of imperial communications to India and latterly because of oil. With the collapse of the Ottoman Empire in 1918, British involvement became more direct with the assumption of League of Nations Mandates over Iraq, Transjordan and Palestine: we already had a controlling interest in Egypt and the Sudan along with a protective relationship with the small states on the perimeter of the Arabian peninsula.

I came to this area as a diplomat in the last period of what Miss Elizabeth Monroe has characterised as 'Britain's Moment in the Middle East'. I served in Iraq when Britain was still the paramount power, in Jordan, Egypt and the Sudan shortly after our influence and power had declined, in Bahrain as the penultimate British Political Agent. I was thus a player in the twilight years of this important glacis of Empire, one step removed from direct rule.

I kept no diaries and have had no access to official papers in writing this book. It is not a detailed record of my Middle Eastern career. I have omitted an account of my years in Palestine and in Turkey as being irrelevant to my central theme. In Palestine I was not a diplomat, and metropolitan Turkey was never a British 'sphere of influence', rather the centre of a great empire. I have already written about Iran in the last years of the Shah. Nor is it yet another attempt to analyse the modern history of the region through British eyes. I have tried to do two things. First, I have done my best to give an impressionistic account of what it was like to serve as a diplomat at varying levels in this unique environment. Second, I have tried to identify the legacy which Britain left to the various countries in which she exercised so much influence for so many years. By revisiting some of the countries in which I had served, I have also attempted to seek out what traces, if any, remain of this legacy today.

I am afraid that many of my contemporaries on the Middle Eastern scene will find my little essay superficial: perhaps it will stimulate them to record their own experiences in greater depth. I trust that I will not give offence to my many Arab friends in whose sense of humour and proportion I have great confidence. Maybe the value, if any, of this book will lie in the future. Some research student in the next century may come across it and find it of use if he or she is trying to reconstruct from documentary evidence something of the flavour of life in the final stages of Britain's Moment.

ONE

Iraq

It was the beginning of the year 1952. The S.S. *Nigaristan*, eight weeks out of London, steamed slowly up the Shatt-el-Arab. Apart from the general cargo, mainly cement for the incipient building boom in the Gulf states, she was carrying my wife, myself and our over-active sons aged two and one, the only passengers. We were en route for the British Embassy in Baghdad. Our relief that the long sea journey was drawing to an end was shared by the ship's officers. In those days there were virtually no berthing facilities for cargo or passenger ships between Aden and Basra and there had been few opportunities to exhaust the children mentally and physically by taking them ashore.

Occasionally we succeeded in begging a lift on a pilot boat or agency launch. On one such occasion we spent an afternoon or two in Kuwait, still a walled town although wealth was beginning to burst through the old mud-brick seams. I recall the contrast between being entertained by the British expatriates at the newly built oil camp at Ahmadi in what they described as 'the best club in the Middle East', and sitting by a muddy creek outside the walls trying unsuccessfully to match a ragged ten-year-old Kuwaiti boy in reciting the Koran.

For weeks the *Nigaristan* had messed about up and down the Gulf, lying off small ports and waiting to unload into lighters which seemed to be permanently contracted to other ships. The children had progressively disposed of their toys, their books, even the ship's chessmen, over the side. A raid on the bridge when the captain was asleep one afternoon had resulted in the destruction of a bundle of charts – perhaps another reason why our journey was so protracted – and the wall-clock in the passengers' saloon

1

had long since lost its hands. Fortunately, in the last stages of our Odyssey, a plague of locusts had driven the children into their cabins in panic-stricken silence, although not before they had seriously depleted the fresh-water supply by turning on the taps of the two baths (with the plugs in) a few hours after the captain had warned us to conserve water: my wife and I only realised the dimensions of the disaster when water started gushing on to the deck from the passages leading to our cabins.

The prospect of the Shatt-el-Arab did not seem to have changed since I had last seen it from the deck of a troopship arriving from Bombay nearly ten years previously. On one side Iran, on the other Iraq, both banks fringed by palm trees, the Iranian shoreline broken by oil installations and the residential compounds of the British officials of the Anglo-Iranian Oil Company. We passed the great Abadan refinery, perhaps Britain's most impressive monument in the whole Middle East. In the early 1940s, on my first passage, it had been in full production, fuelling the Allied war effort. Now it was silent. A few months previously Dr Mossadegh, Prime Minister of Iran, had nationalised Iranian oil, thus extending one of the first major post-war challenges to British supremacy in the area. Now, in 1985, the refinery lies in ruins, destroyed in the fighting between Iran and Iraq.

When I had spent several months in Iraq, Kuwait, Syria, Lebanon, Palestine and Egypt as a junior officer in an artillery regiment in 1943, British power had seemed unchallengeable, something to be taken for granted. We needed no passports, no travel documents, to cross frontiers: a military vehicle and a British uniform were enough. British troops were everywhere, swarming in the bars and night-clubs from Basra to Cairo, deployed in vast camps from the Turkish frontier to the Persian Gulf. Perhaps we did not notice the impermanence of our great, tented cities. Certainly the majority of us, myself included, were unaware of the political stirrings beneath the surface. Our lives touched those of the indigenous inhabitants only superficially, at a level of waiters, bartenders, shopkeepers, night-club hostesses and the Arab workers in our military establishments.

Away from the Europeanised centres of the larger cities, Baghdad, Damascus, Haifa, Beirut, Cairo, Alexandria, the towns were labyrinthine, the villages secretive, hidden from the outsider by mud walls. For the most part we ignored each other, although on the few occasions when I ventured into a small town or village, I invariably encountered courtesy and humour, seldom hostility. I left for the Italian campaign in the autumn of 1943 with my ignorance of the Arab world only slightly dented and with no premonition that I would return shortly and spend most of the remainder of my active life in that region.

Some hours later on that damp day in early 1952, the *Nigaristan* tied up at one of the many berths at the port of Basra. At the head of the gangway my wife and I, carrying the children, said goodbye to the captain. I asked him how much I owed him for the damage the children had done to his ship. 'Major Parsons, just to get your family off my ship is worth more than any money you could give me.' I accepted this valediction without resentment, indeed with some sympathy, and we went ashore.

Basra too looked much the same as when I had first landed there, perhaps from the same gangplank at the same berth. The British military occupation had of course ended with the war but it was still easy to realise that this port at the head of the Persian Gulf, along with Aden far away to the south-west, had lain on the circumference of the circle of power projected by the Indian Empire. The British influence had been filtered through the Britain of Delhi and Bombay: Indian names on shopfronts, British India passenger ships at anchor. The Victorian offices of Scottish trading companies dominated the commercial centre of the town while, in the suburbs, there stretched streets of neat bungalows with deep verandas and substantial gardens, the homes of the expatriate – mainly British – community. We were, inevitably, introduced to the club – entirely British so far as we could see – and I was reassured, in this remote seaport in an independent Arab state, to be told by our hostess at teatime that her husband regretted that he could not be present: he was playing in an important cricket match.

3

My appointment to the Embassy in Iraq as Assistant Military Attaché represented my debut into the world of diplomacy. Nevertheless, since my departure from Egypt for Italy in 1943 I had gained a fair amount of experience of the Middle East. In 1945 I had been seconded to a gendarmerie unit, staffed almost entirely by Arabs. We had first assisted in the evacuation of the French Armed Forces from Syria and had then been stationed in northern Palestine until the termination of the British Mandate in 1948 and the humiliating and ignominious departure of the British military and civilian presence. In Syria and Palestine I had learnt Arabic. After the Palestine débâcle I returned to Oxford University where I read Islamic Studies with Arabic and Turkish as my two languages. The War Office then not unreasonably insisted on a return for their investment. My attempt to resign my commission was turned down and, after some discussion of whether or not, after six years of special duties, I should return to 'proper soldiering', the compromise was reached of appointing me to an attaché post in a country which I knew and with whose language I was by now on familiar terms.

I was returning at a critical time for Britain. The Indian Empire was no more and the Middle East had lost its importance as the line of communication between Britain and the Indian subcontinent. But it had acquired even greater significance as our principal source of crude oil, as an increasingly lucrative export market, even in those far-off days, and as a strategic area under threat from the Soviet Union at the height of the Cold War: Turkey had only recently acceded to the newly formed North Atlantic Treaty Organisation. On the face of it, Britain was still firmly entrenched as the paramount power. From Libya to the borders of Afghanistan, British supremacy was manifest. Britain still ruled the Sudan, Aden and the Aden Protectorates. The Persian Gulf states of Kuwait, Qatar, Bahrain, Oman and what were known as the Trucial States (now the United Arab Emirates) were under British protection. The outside world was disposed to regard Egypt, Jordan and Iraq as little more than client states of Britain. The French position in the Levant had been heavily eroded by France's wartime

experiences, and French influence in her previously man-
dated territories of Syria and Lebanon was at a low ebb. To
the superficial observer, it might have seemed that Britain
had at last won the battle between the European powers for
control over the component parts of the Ottoman Empire,
dismembered by the Allied victory in 1918.

But the foundations of this edifice of influence were beginning to decay. A greater power than Britain was on the
horizon, a nation which, for a combination of commercial
and ideological reasons, was not prepared to contemplate
the continuation of British, or indeed other European, par-
amountcy – the United States of America. The first challenge came in Palestine between 1945 and 1948 when the
American Administration brought irresistible direct and indirect pressure to bear on Britain, combined with overt
support for Zionist aspirations. American control of the
votes of certain small states brought about the adoption by
the General Assembly of the United Nations of the Palestine partition resolution in November 1947, and the state of
Israel was born six months later. The local leaders in the
Arab world and Iran, leaders of communities which, since
the decline in power of the Ottoman and Persian Empires
in the eighteenth century, had relied for their survival and
well-being on their ability to assess the relative strengths
and weaknesses of outside powers, read this portent accurately. Britain was not all-powerful. With this evidence in
mind, and in the reasonable confidence that growing rivalry
between America and Britain for the control of Middle East
oil would ensure a not unsympathetic American reaction to
a breach of Britain's oldest monopoly, Dr Mossadegh
nationalised the Anglo-Iranian Oil Company, precipitat-
ing the Abadan crisis, which was at its height as my family
and I sailed for Basra and Baghdad at the turn of the year
1951–2.

The night train to Baghdad was redolent of a combination
of the Orient Express and the Indian railways of Kipling's
novels. The sleeping car, with its Christian stewards, had
an Ottoman air while the food was British imperial, rice
with most things and Bird's Custard with the rest. When
daylight came we were passing through what appeared to

5

be an endless municipal rubbish heap, dusty and covered with broken pottery – the relics of the ancient world – a route which I had last traversed on an army motor cycle eight or nine years before. At last we drew into Baghdad station. Our new life had begun.

In 1952, the Hashemite Kingdom of Iraq was one of the dominant countries in an Arab world which looked very different from the Arab world of today. The Arab League then comprised only a handful of independent states. Egypt had yet to mobilise its full influence. Syria and the Lebanon had only recently secured their independence from France. Jordan was small, poor and dependent on British financial subsidies. The Saudi kingdom, in the last days of King Ibn Saud, although beginning to realise its oil wealth, was parochial and inward-looking. The remainder of the twenty-odd members of the League of today were still under French or British rule or protection, with the exception of the remote fastness of the Mutawakkilite Imamate of the Yemen.

Iraq, created out of three provinces of the Ottoman Empire as a British Mandate by the Peace Treaties following the First World War, had experienced twenty years of independence. The new state had had a bumpy ride. Diverse in population – Kurds and ethnic Turks in the north, Sunni Arabs in the centre and Shia Arabs in the south – dependent at its outset on the agricultural economy created by the great twin rivers of Tigris and Euphrates, and awarded (by Britain) a monarchy which, notwithstanding its impeccable Arab credentials, had no Iraqi connexions, this was hardly surprising. Iraq had already known internal revolt, military intervention and latterly British invasion when a pro-German regime had briefly seized power in 1941.

However, by the early 1950s, the political and economic landscape looked more promising. The original monarch, King Faisal I, companion of T. E. Lawrence in the Arab Revolt, was long dead. His grandson, King Faisal II, was still a schoolboy at Harrow and the functions of monarchy had for years been exercised by his kinsman, the Regent, Prince Abdulillah. Politics and power were in the hands of a small clique which had grown up as citizens of the Otto-

6

man Empire and had attended the country's birth; tough and skilful men of whom the unchallenged doyen was Nuri Said Pasha, another veteran of the Arab Revolt. Most important, the discovery of oil in northern Iraq and the imminent exploitation of further rich deposits in the south, had transformed the economy and enabled the government to mount a major programme of economic and social development. The prospect of political stability founded on a rapid increase in the prosperity of the mass of the population looked like materialising.

Iraq's standing in outside Arab eyes, and indeed in the eyes of her own population, was heavily coloured by a single factor which had remained constant since the creation of the state – the British connexion. Britain had been midwife at the birth of Iraq. In the ten years of the Mandate, British advisers – names like Arnold Wilson and Gertrude Bell were still common currency thirty years later – had played an important part in creating the administrative and political structures of the new state. Even after the Mandate was terminated and Iraq was accepted as a full member of the League of Nations in 1932, British troops remained in the country under treaty arrangements. English was the only foreign language in common use: successive Iraqi governments automatically looked to Britain for the exploration and exploitation of oil, for the training and organisation of the Armed Forces, for advice on economic development, higher education, public health and much more. By the time I arrived in Baghdad, in spite of the heavy blows to Britain's reputation and prestige dealt by the Palestine fiasco and the nationalisation of the Anglo-Iranian Oil Company, the Iraqi establishment showed no sign of wishing to break this habit of a lifetime, the habit of dependence on British power and British expertise. Time had hallowed a practice which had indeed stood the rulers of Iraq in good stead, and they saw nothing incongruous between their almost symbiotic relationship with Britain and their determination not only to continue to rule their country to the exclusion of the younger and less traditionally minded generation of Iraqis, but also to project Iraq as the leading power in the Arab world.

The British Embassy in Baghdad was heavy with symbolism. An imposing Residence (burnt to the ground in the revolution of 1958) stood alongside a rambling complex of office buildings, the Tigris running along the northern face of the compound, a festering slum to the south. Outside the heavy iron gates stood an equestrian statue of General Sir Stanley Maude (by coincidence a relation of my wife's), the liberator of Baghdad from the Turks in 1917, now the first target of the violent demonstrations which not infrequently swept the city. The other foreign diplomatic missions, even those of the Americans and French, were small and inconspicuous in relation to the British presence, with the possible exception of the Soviet and Nationalist Chinese Embassies who made up in numbers what they lacked in influence.

The modus operandi of the Embassy, under the direction of our wise and experienced Ambassador, Sir John Troutbeck, bore no relation to the façade of archaic imperialism which the compound presented to the world outside. Sir John was sensible of the dilemma facing both Britain and Iraq. Britain needed good relations with Iraq for a variety of practical reasons, strategic, economic and commercial. The Iraqi regime believed that its fortunes were inextricably bound up with those of Britain. So far, so good. But we in the Embassy were conscious that the demonstrable intimacy which this mutuality of interests had created was in itself undermining the foundations of the regime which we needed to sustain. A new and more widely educated generation was growing up, a generation of Iraqis who resented British tutelage, who despised and disliked their rulers for their apparent subservience to Britain, who yearned to break away from what seemed to them to be the stifling embrace of yesterday's imperialism; and who shared the incipient sense of Arab nationalism within a wider unity which was beginning to stir throughout the Levant Arab world. To these people, and there were many of them particularly in the towns and cities, the continuing presence of British Royal Air Force bases at Habbaniya, west of Baghdad, and at Shu'aiba in southern Iraq, was unacceptable; the large number of British experts and advisers, all better

paid and living more luxuriously than their Iraqi counterparts, was a source of resentment; while the conviction that
their rulers were little more than puppets manipulated by
London bred an obsession that the hidden hand of the
British could be discovered behind everything which they
saw as being wrong inside their own country.

Hence, it was our broad strategy, in our direct dealings
with Iraq, to minimise the manifestations which caused resentment and offence and to deal with the Iraqis at all levels
on as normal a basis as possible, thus muffling the overtones
of historical patronage. For example, the Royal Air Force
personnel at Habbaniya and Shu'aiba were discouraged
from visiting the cities of Baghdad and Basra respectively
and forbidden from doing so except in civilian clothes. The
Ambassador, with considerable difficulty, persuaded the
Iraqi leaders, including the Regent and the Prime Minister,
to break the habit of dropping in at the Embassy to discuss
their problems. Such a practice, unheard of in diplomatic
protocol in normal circumstances, only served to confirm
the conviction of the Iraqi people that the British Embassy,
not the Iraqi government, was the true ruler of the country;
the long black cars with their military or police escorts,
turning out of the teeming streets of the suburb of Karkh
into the gates of the Embassy, were scarcely inconspicuous.
The Ambassador insisted instead on behaving as he would
have if accredited to any independent government in the
world; if Ministers or senior officials, a fortiori the Regent
himself, wished to see him, he called on them, not the other
way round. The rest of us were guided by this example.
Our problem was the attitude of our Iraqi interlocutors,
particularly the traditional classes, tribal shaikhs and the
like. The shaikhs, long convinced that their strength de-
rived in great measure from their association with the
British, positively wished to be seen entering the Embassy
on a regular basis by as many people as possible. Fridays
were the days we dreaded for this reason. The weekly holiday for the Iraqi government, it was a working day for the
Embassy. By eleven o'clock in the morning a long line of
Cadillacs, each containing a shaikh with his tribal body-
guard, would be deployed down the Embassy drive, head-

ing for the offices of those of the staff who could talk to them in their own language. The ensuing conversations were usually trivial and inconsequential, but the objective of the shaikhs had been fulfilled: they had been seen refreshing themselves at the well of the great patron.

The Iraqi Armed Forces, with which my admirable boss, Brigadier Arthur Boyce, and I were principally involved, were immediately recognisable as a product of British organisation and training. Almost all their equipment was of British manufacture, and a high proportion of the senior and middle rank officers had been to Sandhurst or Woolwich, or had attended military courses of various kinds in Britain. There were never less than three or four British training teams in Iraq at any one time, engaged either in teaching the Iraqis to use a new item of equipment or in advising on organisational or operational matters such as the conduct of their annual manoeuvres.

In comparison with the huge numbers and the formidable array of modern equipment which Iraq has been able to deploy against Iran in the past five years of war, the Iraqi Armed Forces in my time were tiny. The Army consisted of two infantry divisions plus a brigade of armoured cars (not tanks). The only heavy armour available was a squadron of twelve Churchill tanks, each armed with a disproportionately small gun and capable of a maximum speed of about 10 m.p.h. The Air Force had a front-line strength of about a dozen obsolescent aircraft, while the Navy comprised two river gunboats, built, I think, in Scotland many years previously and manned by artillerymen. There was national conscription but it had become a source of revenue more than of manpower. It was legally possible to buy oneself out of military service for the equivalent of about £100: few except the poorest villagers failed to raise the necessary sum. Interestingly, the Army was recruited and deployed on an ethnic and regional basis: the 1st Division, stationed in the south, was a largely Shia formation, in terms of the rank and file, while the 2nd Division, based in Kurdistan, consisted almost entirely of Kurdish soldiers. Kurds also predominated throughout the officer corps, up to the highest level.

I could not help feeling that the Iraqis had absorbed the outward trappings of a military system which was not necessarily compatible with their national character. British-style organisation and methods were one thing, but the superficial discipline and bearing of the British army sat uneasily on the individualistic and easy-going Iraqi officers. In my first year I must have visited every military station in the country from remote garrisons in the mountains of Kurdistan to dusty, sweltering encampments in the far south. Everywhere it was the same, officers' and sergeants' messes of the British pattern, the neat rows of whitewashed stones surrounding barracks, tents and parade-grounds, vehicles drawn up in precise lines. Was this a mere façade, I wondered, or did it represent a genuine esprit de corps which would be reflected on active service?

At that time Iraq had seldom been tested in battle. But the Army had acquitted itself adequately against internal rebellions, and the units which had fought in the first Arab/Israeli war in 1948 had acquitted themselves not discreditably. In one sense morale amongst the officers was perhaps too high. The Iraqis, I think more so than other Arabs, possessed none of the false modesty so prevalent amongst the English public-school class. There was no question of using that elaborate code of self-deprecation with which the English conceal their true opinion of themselves. In England if the question 'Are you any good at tennis, or golf or cricket?' elicits the reply 'I'm not too bad' or 'I've played a fair amount', this speaks volumes to another Englishman. Not so amongst the Iraqi officer corps. I remember making conversation with a senior officer at a cocktail party shortly after my arrival.

'I understand that you play a good game of polo, Colonel.'

'Of course; with my quick brain and my strong arm, I kick the ball too hard.'

By the same token, the Iraqis had not mastered the art of sportsmanship, a synonym for the ability to accept defeat gracefully. I recall many incidents illustrative of this difference in attitude, some frivolous, others more serious, but all pointing the same moral. There was a somewhat peppery

11

British colonel occupying the post of Chief Instructor at the Iraqi Staff College - Camberley in miniature. He was a fair tennis player and decided to enter the annual Staff College tournament. After several rounds, he reached the finals of the singles to find, to his surprise, that there were three officers including himself in the final round. 'What on earth', he asked the organising committee, 'is Major Ahmad doing in the finals? He was knocked out in the first round.' The reply was short and to the point. 'Do you not know; Major Ahmad is always in the finals!' It was not uncommon for my wife and myself to spend an hour or so knocking up at tennis with Iraqi opponents. If they sensed that they would be beaten, it was impossible to start the proper contest. 'Are you ready?' after ten minutes of knocking up. 'No, let us have a little more practice.' And so on until the allotted time for the match was over. 'We are sorry, we must go now.'

This intense preoccupation with honour could also have deadly consequences. The cream of the Iraqi officer corps, as with their British counterparts, regarded the Staff College as a milestone of military prestige. When I reached Baghdad, the regulation was that, at the end of the course, officers either passed with two years' seniority or with one year's seniority, or they failed. The fact that they had passed the Staff College was marked by a visible symbol - a red flash on the shoulder epaulette. Thus an officer's friends, enemies, rivals and family could tell at a glance whether or not he had achieved the coveted objective or fallen by the wayside. A certain officer failed the final examination. He went to say goodbye to his instructor and embraced him warmly. Simultaneously he pulled out the pin of a grenade which he had hidden under his tunic and blew them both sky high. The popularity of the post of Staff College instructor declined and, with sound common sense, the General Staff decided to change the regulations. From that time forward, officers either passed with two years' seniority or with one year's seniority, or they passed. Everyone emerged with the red flash on his shoulder: honour was satisfied all round and the physical danger inherent in the European approach to examinations was averted.

These characteristics, to British eyes, were not conducive to military efficiency. An obsessive sense of superiority and of personal prestige did not make it easy for the Iraqis to admit that their British advisers or instructors knew more, even about unfamiliar equipment, than their students, and they could have done with more of the English attitude of humility, even if partially false.

As an outside observer, I was in a good position to consider the results of our efforts. They varied, generally in direct proportion to the personal qualities of individual Iraqi commanders. I visited some first-class units, particularly the battalion commanded by the then Lt-Col. Abdul Karim Qasim who was later to lead the bloody coup d'état which overthrew the monarchy and the old regime in 1958. Intense, brooding and highly professional, Qasim was an outstanding officer, with a reputation for courage and leadership in the Arab/Israeli war, and his unit reflected his qualities. The same was true of other officers in key positions, many of whom emerged as members of the group who planned and executed the 1958 coup.

Elsewhere the standard was less impressive. I remember observing a divisional artillery exercise somewhere near Babylon, south of Baghdad. The gun drill of the artillerymen was exact and rigid, according to the British pattern: the transmission of orders would have done credit to the School of Artillery at Larkhill. But the shells were flying in all directions except at their targets. The whole affair eventually dissolved into chaos. Two memories remain. First of walking across a field of potsherds with a group of officers, one of whom suddenly bent down and picked up an exquisite Babylonian figurine of a woman, a reminder that the shells were landing in an area which had known civilisation for thousands of years. Secondly, on my return to Baghdad, I naively gave my American colleague a copy of my report to the War Office on the exercise. He passed it straight to the Iraqi Director of Artillery, who could not bring himself to speak to me for months. This was my first and most salutary taste of Anglo-American competition in Iraq. I learnt my lesson.

I also recall a visit which my wife and I paid to the Navy

- the two gunboats - which were anchored on the Tigris at the town of Amara in south-east Iraq. (I sometimes wondered why the Americans needed two Naval Attachés to cover this armada.) It was midsummer and the temperature stood at about 120° in the shade. We set off in our battered Humber Hawk before dawn for a nine-hour drive down the dust track which led to Kut (of First World War fame) and then to Amara. To open the car windows meant suffocation from the dust which billowed around us. To keep them closed meant roasting alive. We alternated between these two forms of death for a few hours, when I noticed that my wife had lost consciousness. I drove across the desert to the river and drenched her in muddy water. She revived and we continued, in the ominous knowledge that a formal luncheon lay ahead of us at which we would be expected to be not only well dressed but on our best behaviour.

We arrived at last, two exhausted pillars of dust, and were led to our quarters on one of the gunboats. It was immaculate, all white paint and gleaming brass. But the water which emerged from the shower was mud and the refrigerator, on which we fell like Saharan travellers dying of thirst, turned out to contain only a roll of lavatory paper - a considerate concession to our European habits.

Our reception could not have been kinder or more friendly, but I cannot claim that the naval aspect of the visit was a success. The Commanding Officer had arranged a cruise up-river during the afternoon and evening. We set off in style - I sensed that it was the first time that the gunboat had left its moorings for some months - and enjoyed some convivial hours on deck. The radio emitted interminable Arabic songs. At one point my wife asked one of the officers what the singer was saying. 'It is a love song. She is saying - "I am on the fire".' My wife and I looked at each other in the sudden realisation that we and the singer had something in common. There was a powerful smell of burning on deck, too penetrating to be ignored. The water-cooling intake had sucked in quantities of river mud and the overheated engines had seized up. Furious activity followed while we enjoyed the romance of the Tigris in the moonlight. Hours later we returned to Amara on the second gunboat, which had been summoned to the rescue. It had been a long, but entertaining, day.

For all the welcoming bonhomie, the determined professionalism and the self-assurance, I was conscious of a thread of frustration and discontent running through the fabric of the armed forces. When the Egyptian Free Officers overthrew the monarchy in June 1952, expelled King Farouk from the country and established a new order, the suppressed desire to follow suit was palpable, particularly amongst the majors and colonels. My Iraqi colleagues were hospitable men and I spent many evenings in the Baghdad officers' club or in garrison messes. The conversations, especially after heavy potations of the local arak or of mahogany-coloured whiskies and water, would frequently turn to politics, a favourite subject being their attitude towards the British and to what they regarded as their own British-sponsored government. The more radical officers, such as Abdul Karim Qasim and others whom I could name but will not – they may still be alive – would argue that all Iraq's ills stemmed from the regime. Get rid of it and the problems arising from poverty, ignorance, dependence on foreigners, ethnic diversity, etc., would disappear. Others were more cautious, critical of the ageing men who had been running the country since the 1920s, envious of the advent to power of young men elsewhere in the Arab world, ardent for reform. These people felt somehow suffocated by the conservatism of monarchist Iraq, and longed to burst into a freer and wider landscape.

As officers they were conscious of the contempt with which the Iraqi civilian establishment regarded the armed services. Their social prestige was low. There were exceptions, but the majority of the officer corps was drawn from the urban shopkeeper or minor official class, not from the great families. They were not well paid nor did they receive generous fringe benefits. Service away from the capital could be long, hard and uncomfortable. Their equipment was sparse and obsolescent. In a nutshell they were made aware of their lack of élite and favoured status in the country.

They regarded their exclusive British connexion with

15

mixed feelings. There was no lack of genuine personal affection – I made many good friends – and several of them
had thoroughly enjoyed their times in England: a few had
married British girls. They respected our military capability
and admired much in the British way of life. An important
minority, however, could never forgive us for the humiliating treatment they had received at the pre-war military col-
leges of Sandhurst and Woolwich. These men nurtured an
unquenchable hatred of the gross horseplay and racial ar-
rogance to which they had been exposed in late adolescence.
At least one such officer, who became a friend of mine – we
shared a common interest in modern Iraqi poetry – played
a leading part in the 1958 coup.

But they also felt restricted by their dependence on
British equipment, training and advice. It was not so much
that they thought that we were inferior to other potential
suppliers; rather that their relationship with Britain
smacked too much of tutelage. They would have liked to
experiment, to broaden their contacts, to try something and
someone new. Naturally enough these longings were being
warmly fostered by our competitors, the United States and
France in particular, less so by the Soviet Union whose
influence in Iraq at the time was marginal to put it at its
highest.

Furthermore, events in Palestine were beginning to permeate the thinking of the armed forces, as was the case with
civilian and military society throughout the Arab world. I
visited many officers' messes the walls of which were hung
with plaques recording casualties in Palestine (somewhat
exaggerated by the fact that, as I noticed after a while, the
name of any man who had been killed also appeared, with
some logic, in the lists of those lightly wounded and heavily
wounded), and it was a favourite topic of conversation. We,
the British, could not be forgiven for abandoning our responsibilities and it was hard to explain to the Iraqis how
it was that the nation which they had been brought up to
regard as all-powerful had been so humiliated by a combination of American and Jewish pressure.

By 1952, this growing preoccupation with Palestine, combined with Iraq's close links with Britain, was beginning to

infect the domestic health of the regime and to inhibit its bid for leadership of the Arab world. With the inspiration of the revolution in Egypt, the infection spread. However, the handful of men who had taken turns to rule Iraq for thirty years seemed on the face of it to be in control. But they were not popular and the Regent, elegant, etiolated and avid to retain the power which he had acquired years before through the death of his cousin King Ghazi, in a car accident, was universally disliked: rumours about his private life and the corruption of the Palace clique were as thick as leaves in autumn. He was not even respected as a politician. Not so with old Nuri Said Pasha who generated both awe and fear in his mastery of the Iraqi political game, skilfully balancing his alliance of political cronies, tribal shaikhs and provincial grandees. Old-fashioned and openly contemptuous of the new forces arising round him, he was a man who radiated strength and resolution: his presence in a room overshadowed all others. The remainder of the political establishment were, with exceptions, men of the same stamp and the same generation. Sometimes in power, sometimes out of office, sometimes in favour with Nuri, sometimes in his bad books, they were the Boodles and Coodles of a political sham which Charles Dickens would have recognised without difficulty.

There was a so-called democratic structure, based on a British-style constitution, complete with political parties. The citizens of Eatenswill would have found it familiar, a vehicle designed to disarm foreign critics and to facilitate the periodic shuffling of the small pack of cards, rather than to express in any serious way the will of the people. There were legitimate opposition parties outside the little cluster of Ins and Outs, but they were kept on a tight rein and given no chance at general elections. These periodic exercises in democracy generated a compound of frustration, anger and ridicule. Ballot-rigging was made easy by the high rate of illiteracy, the rule being that the officials at the polling stations wrote down on the voting papers the names which the illiterate voters had chosen. If the opposition candidate was named Mohammed and the government candidate was Ahmad, the officials simply wrote in Ahmad

17

regardless of how many of the electorate opted for Mohammed.

From time to time the government had recourse to subtler methods. A friend of mine, a regular officer in the Army, a man of high intelligence and considerable strength of character, decided to resign his commission in order to contest the 1953 general election in his native city of Kirkuk. He was standing for an opposition party of which the government, for no particularly good reason, disapproved. I said goodbye to him a few days before he left to campaign in the constituency. A week or so later we met by chance in the street in Baghdad. I asked him why he was not canvassing the electorate in Kirkuk, a few hundred miles away. He told me his story. The government had issued a regulation that there would be no public meetings during the election campaign. He had no intention of defying this rule. But, the day after he arrived in Kirkuk, he had been walking down a street on his way to visit a friend. He had cigarettes but no matches. He stopped and asked a couple of passers-by for a light. A policeman jumped out of the bushes and accused him of holding a public meeting, adding that if he stayed in Kirkuk, he would be arrested for defying the law. He returned to Baghdad, a defeated man, his military commission sacrificed, his political career over before it had started.

Hardly surprising, therefore, that, in such an environment, the people of Iraq regarded riot and civil disorder as the only effective means of bringing pressure to bear on the government. This happened in 1948 when the government concluded an unpopular treaty with Britain. The charade of a parliament being irrelevant, serious rioting broke out and the treaty had to be annulled. The same thing happened in 1952. I forget the specific causes but the government of the day had become intensely unpopular. Suddenly the streets filled with surging crowds. Some policemen were doused with petrol and burnt: the streets emptied of police. Needless to say, although the causes of the disturbance were entirely domestic, the British Embassy was one of the first targets. A crowd gathered outside, focusing on the traditional target of the Baghdad mob, the equestrian statue of

18

General Maude. For a time it looked as if the gates might be stormed. We told the Ambassador that the situation looked unpromising. 'Ah,' he said, 'I see. Our prestige has become dangerously high again!'

The Americans too had one of their first tastes of rising prestige. I remember driving my car to the Ministry of Defence and passing the United States Information Centre as it was being looted and destroyed. Rioters were throwing packets of dollar bills – why dollars in Iraq, I wondered? – out of the windows of the Centre to their friends in the street.

For two or three days there was anarchy in the streets of Baghdad. The army was called in and the rioting subsided to some extent. But it was clear that the conscript soldiers were not prepared to fire on their civilian compatriots. The military patrols were treated with a certain amount of respect but I saw a Churchill tank being used in the main street as a platform from which leaders of the riots addressed their supporters: the tank crew made no attempt to prevent them. After some days of this strange situation, during which normal movement in the city was impossible, the government's unpopular measures were rescinded and the Prime Minister was replaced by the Chief of the General Staff, General Nuruddin Mahmoud. The crisis passed although, shortly afterwards, General Nuruddin was manoeuvred out of office and into retirement by the Boodles and Coodles, a personal humiliation which did not pass unnoticed by the officer corps.

For a brief moment in 1953, it looked as though the appearance and the reality of the Iraqi political scene might merge into a national unity which could disperse the miasma of disaffection. The young King, Faisal II, returned from England where he had been educated from infancy. He had reached the age of eighteen and the time had come for him to be crowned and to assume the functions of monarchy. The coronation ceremonies were magnificent, attended by dignitaries from many countries. More important, the occasion created an air of expectation amongst the people of Baghdad that a new era was dawning. The King was an unimpressive figure, short and already overweight.

But he was young and new, and hope ran through the country (shared by the Embassy) that the Regent would withdraw from the scene and that the younger generation would be given their opportunity. For the first and only time, I sensed an atmosphere of genuine warmth, contrasting with the sullen acquiescence or blatant sycophancy with which the Royal Family was customarily regarded. Even the old Communist poet, Mohammed Mahdi el Jawaihiri, was prevailed upon to deliver a public eulogy of the King, who responded in imperfect Arabic.

But, as the coronation celebrations ended and normal life resumed, our optimism declined. There was no doubt of the King's desire to do well by his people. However, his public appearances had revealed his shyness and lack of the tough, soldierly qualities which already distinguished his cousin, King Hussein of Jordan. As the two little figures sat on adjoining thrones it was easy to detect which of them was the more likely to command loyalty and respect. Faisal looked miserable throughout, his mood lightening only in the company of the small group of British schoolfriends from Harrow who had been flown out as his guests. The Regent, now Crown Prince only, treated him with avuncular patronage and, as the weeks and months passed, showed no sign of surrendering the powers to which he had grown accustomed over seventeen years. The illusion of impending change faded.

Meanwhile, the surplus oil revenues were being applied to a sensible programme of economic development, too sensible perhaps. The Development Board was dominated by British advisers, mainly men who had gained their expertise in India and other parts of the Empire. Their attitude to development, prudent and full of common sense, matched the natural instincts of the Iraqi ruling clique. British contractors and consulting engineers were busy implementing (almost always behind time) projects for road building in remote areas, for hydro-electric and irrigation dams in the far mountains of Kurdistan, for flood prevention schemes which would for ever free southern Iraq from the danger of inundation which had plagued the country since the days of Noah. The government, contemptuous of the politician's art of currying favour with the people, took no trouble to publicise the future benefits of these schemes, and would have nothing to do with glamorous but developmentally unsound ventures such as slum clearance and low-cost housing. Socially, there was security of a kind, but the urban masses were still sunk in the ignorance and squalor of previous centuries. Even in education, the former capital of the Abbasid Empire, which had stretched from Spain to India, did not boast a University, only a Higher Teachers Training College. There was a University project in gestation but I remember a distinguished British professor telling me that it was something of a waste of time and effort: 'The Iraqis are not really ready for a University.'

So the people as a whole, conscious that they were citizens of one of the wealthiest states in the Arab world, saw no direct and immediate benefit from the tens of millions of dinars which they knew to be flowing annually into the Treasury; and were disposed to conclude that the bulk of this money must be going into the pockets of the already rich and already powerful. Indeed some of it was, but it is beyond argument that homeric work was in hand to lay the infrastructural foundations of a prosperous modern state. A regime of a totally different nature, having slaughtered or imprisoned most of those who held power in my time, would reap the rewards.

But life was not entirely a matter of politics and economics. It was good to be young and British and official in the Iraq of those days, over thirty years ago. Kipling would have recognised us as latter-day players in a slightly suburban, slightly déclassé production of the Raj. There were the clubs, Alwiya (pretentious) and Railway (despised by Alwiya), around which the pleasures of the expatriates largely revolved. They too had their social hierarchies, their intrigues – I remember an over-stimulated English lady shooting the Alwiya Club Secretary in the leg one evening on account of some real or fancied misdemeanour – their Scottish dances, tea, tennis courts, the swimming pool around which women would play bridge from nine o'clock in the morning. There was the intense heat in the infancy of air-conditioning, alleviated by nights under mosquito

21

nets on the flat roof of our cavernous, old Turkish house on the banks of the Tigris, long siestas in the cool semi-underground rooms, ceiling fans creaking and a breeze from the river blowing through damp camelthorn screens fastened to the windows: long nights when sleep was impossible, spent in the garden night-clubs with whisky and grotesque cabarets until dawn sent us off to breakfast and our offices – only until half past one, when all work ceased for the day.

Unlike Kipling's India Baghdad was healthy and our children flourished in the pools and playgrounds, unmoved by temperatures of over 115°. The older British children went home early to preparatory and public schools, but ours remained in the company of our Chaldean nanny, her English vocabulary redolent of association with British troops in wartime, and went to the excellent school run by the British Council, principally for Iraqi children. I suppose, looking back, that the two schools then operated in Baghdad by the Council played as large a part as any or all British institutions in creating Anglophilia amongst the future generation of Iraqis and their young parents. It was notable that they even survived the revolution of 1958: some of the leaders of the coup had children at them and regarded them with respect.

There were more vigorous sports as well. The Royal Harithiya Hunt (jackals) complete with a Master, whippers-in, pink coats, officers in uniform (one of them, overcome with the excitement of the chase, once rode ahead of the hounds and shot the jackal with his revolver) provided a major social occasion, patronised as it was by the Regent himself: even an annual Hunt Ball. For the less ambitious, those like myself who can only ride to save their lives, there was shooting – wild boar, black partridge, duck; dawn on the marshes, evenings in the date gardens, weekends spent with shaikhs whose houses, miles from the nearest habitation, seemed to have been copied from the kind of holiday homes to be found disfiguring every seaside town in south-east England. I remember one such occasion when, after a seven-hour drive over a corrugated dusty track, my wife and I arrived at one of these little stucco palaces in a great waste of a fallow, alluvial plain. 'Have a bath before we start shooting,' said the Shaikh hospitably. 'We would love to,' we replied from behind our heavy coating of dust. We were shown into a splendid bathroom, equipped with a sunken marble bath with what appeared to be gold taps, a bidet and wash-basin similarly accoutred. The only problem was that the pipes ended at the wall: there was no water supply within a hundred miles. Seeing our predicament, a tribesman entered the room carrying a small basin and a smaller jug of water with a long spout. He poured the water over our hands and we removed the worst of the dust. When we rejoined the Shaikh for tea, prior to the slaughter of hundreds of black partridge, we congratulated him on the magnificence of his bathroom. We naturally said nothing about the trifling matter of the absence of water.

And the travelling itself; bounding across the endless, lion-coloured, alluvial deserts of the south and west: the stony plains north to Kirkuk and Mosul: the long slow train which bisected the country from north to south: always there was a railway rest-house (shades of India again) for the night, comfortable, liberally supplied and usually staffed by an ancient gentleman who would pull from his robes a great pile of chits and references signed by long-dead Englishmen half a century ago. Kurdistan was, I think, our favourite province. The country was at peace with itself in those days and a British official could travel to every corner of it. The excellent Iraqi State Railways had begun to build holiday bungalows and hotels in the mountains. Cold and clear after the dusty plains, twinkling at night with the lights of villages and shepherds' fires, these mountains were enchanted places. Green rice fields gave way to rocky ravines and tree-covered slopes: in the far north where we once camped for a week in a Royal Air Force tented leave centre, where the frontiers of Iraq, Turkey and Iran meet, the Kurdish and Christian villages and villagers were indistinguishable except that in one village the highest building was topped by a cross, in another by a crescent: there was snow on the heights even in mid-summer.

Even in that Shangri-La the absurd pursued us. Our

23

policy of keeping the British Armed Services under cover had paid off to the extent that the wife of a senior Air Force officer once asked us if we met many Egyptians in our job. We replied that we met the Embassy staff but that they were only a handful. She looked puzzled until it dawned on us that, with a Field Post Office address common to the Suez Canal Zone and Iraq, she had spent her time in Habbaniya under the impression that she was in Egypt. I explained the difference with all the tact I could muster.

Yes, we may have been part of a system of 'imperialist hegemony' and we may have sensed that violent change could not be far away. But we still look back with nostalgia on Iraq in the early 1950s and on our many Iraqi friends, officers, officials, teachers, poets, all welcoming and courteous to myself and my family.

After two years in Iraq, we returned to London. I had transferred to the Diplomatic Service in which I was to spend the rest of my active career and ahead of us lay a year at the Foreign Office, followed by a four-year posting to the Embassy in Ankara. We left in the spring of 1954, a time of drama and tragedy for Baghdad and the surrounding countryside. Iraq was experiencing the worst floods for many years and the city was completely cut off except by air. Flying over Baghdad in a light aeroplane, I could see nothing but water as far as the horizon, except for little huddled villages and herds of goats and cattle on patches of higher ground a few feet above the floods. The loss in livestock and crops must have been immense and many people must have drowned. From time to time the flood barriers around the city had to be breached (to save the date gardens of the pashas as the rumour ran) destroying the mud huts of the very poor. Everywhere people were filling and carrying sandbags. The political temperature rose as the weeks passed with no relief and no escape. Rumours proliferated and, ironically, no one appeared to realise that this natural disaster, so familiar to the people of the Tigris and Euphrates, was happening for the last time. One of the major development schemes, in the Wadi Tharthar basin some miles north of Baghdad, would shortly be completed and there would be no more floods.

It was at the time of my departure that my favourite rumour originated, an incident whose quality illustrates the complex mythology which lay beneath the surface of the Iraqi-British relationship, and appropriately closes this account. One of the leading Baghdad newspapers published a report one day that the British were infiltrating diseased prostitutes from the R.A.F. camp at Habbaniya into the city in order to corrupt the health of the noble Iraqi youth. I met the editor a few days later and suggested to him that he had gone too far. We were used to verbal and written attacks and, I hoped, took them in good part, but this particular story was, in my opinion, offside. He laughed and admitted that he and his staff had invented it on a hot evening in the office. Then he paused and added, 'Yet, you know, a lot of my readers believe it; so maybe there is something in it after all!'

Thirty years later

For years I have been told that the old Kuwait has long been buried under mountains of money. Our arrival in December 1984 by jumbo jet of Gulf Aviation into the cavernous halls and corridors of Kuwait International Airport certainly differs from our landing from a pilot boat off the S.S. *Nigaristan* at a small and barnacled jetty thirty years before. Then, we were within a few yards of the centre of the town: now we drive twenty miles past floodlit international road signs intersecting with six concentric circles of ring-roads.

Yes, thirty years of accumulating wealth have transformed Kuwait from a small town, hemmed in between the desert and the Gulf, into a vast featureless expanse of low houses, punctuated in the middle by a cluster of high buildings, which we observe from the viewing platform of a vertiginous tower some hundreds of feet high. No doubt the general level of prosperity is as high as the tower. But a search of the city reveals some traces of bygone days. Bits of the old city wall have been preserved and I eventually identify, now buried by a car park alongside a large department store, the spot where I exchanged Koranic quotations with the small Kuwaiti boy, who must now be middle-aged, when we entertained our small children by the muddy creek on our way to the same destination, Baghdad, at the outset of our diplomatic career. We are also just ahead of the bulldozers which are about to demolish the last remaining part of the old covered bazaar: old men are still slapping down backgammon pieces in outdoor cafés. On the last day of our three-day visit we drive sixty miles into the desert to picnic with the Ambassador and his wife. The city peters out in the familiar Arab wilderness of small cafés, garages and workshops: soon we see the black tents of nomads herding sheep and goats on the bare, dun-coloured hills which stretch to the border with Iraq. On our return, passing a large flock of flamingoes happily stabbing with their beaks the sewage alongside an indescribably filthy beach, we see more futuristic buildings: the new National Assembly facing a small shanty town on a beach swarming with children and flies buzzing over rotting carcases of fish: an imposing office block stares into another relic of the past, the Amir's Palace. Old derelict houses crumble by steel and glass bank buildings. Even in this quintessential oil shaikhdom, a welfare state par excellence, where there is little left to develop even with all the money available, the tenacious past still confronts the plutocratic present. The Kuwaiti people themselves, although now a minority amongst foreign immigrants, look and behave much as always. Their material circumstances may be beyond the dreams of their grandparents but their traditions, their basic way of life, have remained intact.

It is evening again, 7th December 1984, and the aircraft of Kuwait Airways is landing at the new airport at Baghdad, some miles from its small, primitive predecessor with its snipe marsh at the end of the runway. The terminal building, constructed especially for the Summit Meeting of the Non-Aligned Movement which, had it not been for the Iran/Iraq war, would have been held in Baghdad in 1982, is brobdingnagian in extent and ultra-modern in design, great aluminium stalactites depending from the roof far above.

Any visitor to Iraq today who entertains doubts regarding

the identity of the President of the Republic is quickly and convincingly enlightened. The airport is named Saddam International: throughout the city and at regular intervals on the roads into the countryside 10-foot-square placards of President Saddam Hussein are displayed. To add variety, on the principle of something for everyone, the leader is depicted in a multitude of different characterisations – the fierce warrior, the homely peasant, the general brooding over the panorama of battle, the dreamy academic, the tough but genial chairman of committees, are only some of the representations which I recall.

But these works of art are invisible as our car rushes us from the airport in the darkness along a broad motorway at 100 m.p.h. to a grand hotel, also built for the Non-Aligned Summit which never took place, where we are deposited in a luxurious and comfortable suite. In the morning we look out of the window at a broad expanse of garden with a vista of trees and modern buildings beyond. 'Where can we be?' my wife asks. 'This could be many modern cities in the world: it certainly isn't Baghdad.'

By evening we are beginning to get our bearings. Our friendly hosts from the Foreign Ministry have given us a comprehensive tour of the city. Baghdad has grown from a small city strung out on both banks of the Tigris to a great conurbation of some 4 million population – there cannot have been more than 500,000 in my time. The West Bank has been transformed out of all recognition from a narrow strip of old houses (where we used to live) into an expanse of public buildings, residential areas and broad boulevards reaching deep into what had been virgin country dotted with date palm plantations. Only the heart of the city is familiar. There has been much renovation and new construction but Rashid Street, the centre of Baghdad, is more or less the same as before and, around the golden mosque of Kadhimain, the shops and bazaars, the people, are as they were over thirty years ago: amongst the taxis, broken-down horse-drawn carriages – the arabanas of old Baghdad – jog slowly along. As in Kuwait and Bahrain, the tenacious past is still holding on: even the Alwiya Club, now with almost entirely Iraqi membership, survives!

27

We visit the Embassy. The old slum of Karkh is being cleared and new, tall buildings are rising from ground freed of the previous huddle of mud-brick shops. The end of the Embassy garden has been sliced off and the equestrian statue of my wife's cousin, General Maude, has long disappeared. Inside the walls nothing much has changed except that the Ambassador's Residence, burnt down in 1958, is no longer there; only an empty and weed-grown pediment separates the office building from what used to be the ballroom, now the Embassy staff club, reminiscent of a sergeants' mess. The offices are the same old jumble of rooms and courtyards, upstairs galleries, half-underground cellars. I even find my old room, at the top of the same rickety flight of stairs. Workmen are busy patching, redecorating, holding it all together. Fitzgerald would have gone straight to the point: 'They say the Lion and the Lizard keep/The courts where Jamshyd gloried and [particularly at the annual Queen's Birthday Party] drank deep.'

Iraq today is a country at war. Foreign exchange is carefully husbanded and, although the necessities of life are adequate, imports are limited and the shops – even the boutiques in our hotel – are austere and half-empty. Banners across street and on walls proclaim the heroism of martyrdom. Cabinet Ministers and senior members of the ruling Ba'ath Party wear the battledress of the People's Militia, pistols slung at their hips: some of the Ministers, those with military backgrounds, look more capable of using their weapons than others. The city and its military garrisons are encircled by anti-aircraft defences. Nevertheless there are still plenty of young men in civilian clothes in the streets and, apart from the Militia, military uniforms are rare – rarer than they were in the time of peace when we served in Iraq.

We revisit the site of the ancient city of Babylon, about sixty miles south of Baghdad. The countryside, the agriculture, looks much the same; evidence of mechanisation is sparse, confined to the occasional tractor. The small towns and villages through which we pass have yet to be touched by the hand of modernity. The people could be the same as those whom I used to see during my frequent visits to military garrisons in this area long ago. We arrive at Babylon to be shown round the site by an attractive and well-informed young Iraqi lady. At the entrance, my attention is caught by a sign in Arabic which, in translation, reads as follows: 'O visitor, smile for the eternal city of Babylon: smile for Hammurabi, the great law-giver: smile for Nebuchadnezzar, the conqueror of tyranny: smile for Saddam Hussein, the victorious leader.' The young lady and I look at each other impassively as I translate this stimulating message aloud for my wife's benefit.

We fly back to London on an almost empty jumbo jet of Iraqi Airways, our three-day return to Baghdad at an end. I try to collect my impressions. Our hosts have treated us with the kindness and hospitality which is characteristic of the Arab world. We have not been made to feel like well-treated prisoners. We have been shown everything we have asked to see: no attempt has been made to confine our tours of the city and the country to the modern, spectacular sights. The physical changes which I have seen are greater in certain respects than I had anticipated, less in others. Much of the past has survived revolution and the wealth which oil has brought: the traditional Iraqi way of life clearly persists. And yet the political change has been absolute. In the old days of the monarchy, the ramshackle attempt to combine Western (specifically British) constitutionalism with Ottoman authoritarianism was effective only in proportion to the strength of personality of a handful of powerful individuals. Nuri Said and his colleagues were elderly men by my time and were clinging to power with all the political skills at their command in the hope that rising economic prosperity would outrun political discontent. The governing establishment lacked legitimacy in the eyes of the people and even the sense of Iraqi nationhood was weak. There was no ideology or party organisation to mobilise or to coerce the masses into obedience or active support. In the background lurked the Armed Forces with their history of political intervention, distempered by social inferiority and poor conditions of service, excited by the achievements of their brother officers in Egypt, expected to give loyalty *à l'anglaise* to 'king and country', a foreign king in a country which, in the eyes of some, scarcely existed. The only way in which popular dissatisfaction could be expressed was through violence, and the chances always were that this violence would one day find a military leader who would strike home. In retrospect, the Suez affair was probably the death knell of the Hashemite regime. By failing to break with his British allies who had invaded a sister Arab country in collusion with Israel, the ultimate enemy, Nuri Said had fatally compromised the regime in the eyes of the Armed Forces and indeed of all elements of opposition, even neutrally disposed people, in Iraq. The fact that the reaction was slow to come made the old gentlemen in power complacent and careless. On the 14th July 1958 they allowed the only armoured unit in the Armed Forces, with its arms and ammunition, to pass through Baghdad. The inevitable happened and the always fragile house of cards was swept away in a few hours. Ten years of uncertainty followed. The author of the 1958 coup, Abdul Karim Qasim, was himself assassinated in 1963: military leader replaced military or civilian leader as the Iraqi nationalists and the pan-Arabs fought for control. In 1968 the Ba'ath Socialist Party consolidated its hold and the same group of people, or most of them, have remained in power ever since.

It is dangerous to use the word stability in relation to states where there is no established tradition of institutional continuity in the nature of government. Who for example in the 1940s could have foreseen the tidal wave of pan-Arab nationalism which so nearly swept the Middle Eastern board only ten years later? By the same token, who in the turbulent 1950s and 1960s could have anticipated that, twenty years later, this tide would have ebbed, leaving the traditional regimes of Jordan and the Arabian peninsula firmly entrenched? Chance and the impulsive actions of individuals are more potent forces for sudden change than in, say, Western Europe. However, with due regard to these uncertainties, Iraq 1984 displays more evidence of future continuity than Iraq 1954. The war with Iran has taken a grim toll of lives, but the Iraqi reaction to it over more than four years has demonstrated a degree of national solidarity which would have been astonishing thirty years ago. With few exceptions, the disparate communities which make up the state have fought as Iraqis, particularly in defence of the national territory. The Kurds have not seized the opportunity to make a successful bid for separation; nor have the Shias rallied to their sectarian co-religionists in Tehran.

Furthermore the Ba'ath Party has provided the ideological and organisational framework for which other Arab governments, such as Nasser's Egypt, sought in vain. The Party, with the small and closely knit Revolutionary Command Council at its head, dominates the newly elected National Assembly. Party cells operate in all cities, towns and villages, and permeate the military and civilian governmental apparatus. Discipline is stern and implacable: woe betide 'enemies of the state'. The cult of President Saddam Hussein is bizarre to Western eyes, but Iraq is Iraq, not Sweden. Since the eighth century, the people of Iraq have had a reputation for violence and sedition. The Shia rebellion against the first, Omayyad, Caliphate originated in Iraq and the Iraqis were the only Arab people who revolted bloodily against the imposition of a British Mandate in 1920. The Iraqi people have historically responded to firm, individual leadership: they have such leadership now, allied to an all-watching, all-seeing party organisation. It is not easy to imagine a colonel with a handful of tanks seizing the radio station and toppling the present regime as happened so frequently throughout the region twenty years or so ago.

What of the British, the literal power behind the throne of bygone days, of my first tour of duty in Baghdad? It is rash to pontificate after a three-day visit as a guest of the government. But, apart from the allegations about British arms supplies to Iran, I came away with the impression that much of the past has been buried. I found none of the paranoia which I experienced in Iran where, even in the late 1970s, the hidden hand of Britain was seen behind everything, even the revolution which brought down the Shah. The Embassy is severely restricted in its contacts but so are all diplomatic missions in Baghdad. British cultural diplomacy is active and welcomed: the British Council centre which I visited was packed with Iraqi students, reading, studying or just chatting to each other. There are more

Iraqi post-graduate students in Britain than there are from any other country in the world. What was best in our past association seems to have survived, a kind of affinity based on long association, expressing itself now in the fact that Iraqis still probably feel more at home in Britain than they do in any other non-Middle Eastern foreign country.

And Britain is of course not all that important to the present Iraqi leadership. We have found our level in their eyes, far below that of the two superpowers – the resumption of full diplomatic relations with the United States had been consummated shortly before our visit – less interesting militarily than France (now a major supplier of arms to Iraq), less attractive economically than West Germany or Japan. Britain is perceived as a middle-rank European power, not even as a potential leader of the European Community. Our experience in the Middle East gains us some respect and our past in Iraq is still alive in people's minds to the extent that it is difficult for them to regard us with wholly neutral eyes. But the chips on the shoulder are scarcely visible, if at all; an equality of relationship has, after so many years, been achieved, ironically when it matters less to both sides than at any time since we assisted at the birth of the Iraqi state over sixty years ago.

TWO

Jordan

'I hate the French.'

'Oh, really.'

'And I hate the Americans twice as much as I hate the French.'

'How interesting.'

'But my combined hatred of the French and the Americans is nothing to my hatred of the British!'

The old Jerusalem journalist, an Egyptian who had come to Palestine as a young man in the wake of Field-Marshal Allenby's armies in 1917, leant back in his chair and looked hard at my wife. They had not met before. We were lunching with him and other Arab newspapermen at the hotel in East Jerusalem which had been his home for many years. I was at the time (1959) a First Secretary in the Embassy in Amman and it was part of my job to spend a couple of days every week on the West Bank, mainly to keep up our contacts with the local authorities and the local information media. The principal Arabic newspapers were in those days published in Jerusalem and my old acquaintance was the leading columnist of a paper which was as hostile as it dared to be to the Hashemite dynasty and their British and American allies.

For a moment I wondered how my wife would cope with this sally. We had been out of the Arab world for the previous five years, which we had spent in the Embassy in Ankara, and I thought that she might have lost her touch in dealing with such exchanges. I need not have worried. 'What a relief,' she replied. 'For a second I thought you were going to be complimentary about us. That would have given me a shock. It's good to know that nothing has changed while we have been away.' The old man burst into

33

roars of laughter in which the rest of us joined. The meal proceeded to the accompaniment of conversation on the two topics which overshadowed all others in Jordan in the 1950s – Nasserism and the Palestine problem.

A great volume of water had flowed under many political and military bridges since we had left Iraq five years earlier. Gamal Abdul Nasser's version of secular, socialist, republican Arab nationalism, fiercely non-aligned in foreign policy and dedicated to the extirpation of imperialism (Britain and France) and its stooges (Arab regimes still in close relationship with those powers), was sweeping the Arab world. From Morocco to the Persian Gulf, monarchs, shaikhs and amirs were trembling on their thrones. A year previously, the Hashemite monarchy in Iraq had gone down in blood to a coup d'état which owed much to the inspiration of Nasserism, and Iraq was now ruled by a group of wild republican officers, already divided between Iraqi nationalists and those who favoured immediate union with Egypt. Syria and Egypt had merged in the United Arab Republic, leaving Jordan surrounded by hostile powers on all fronts. The Baghdad Pact, an attempt by Britain, Iraq and Turkey to forge an alliance which would replace the anachronistic Anglo-Iraqi treaty relationship, had been emasculated by the defection of revolutionary Iraq. And there had been another major round of Arab/Israeli warfare. In 1956 the Israelis had invaded Sinai concurrently with an Anglo/ French assault on the Suez Canal Zone, Nasser having nationalised the Canal Company six months previously. The Israelis had been forced back to their frontier by American pressure and the Suez affair had finally exploded the myth of British omnipotence in the region. British prestige had plummeted. Seen by the majority including myself as immoral and inexpedient (if an objective had been to topple Nasser, the result had been to make him a hero), and demonstrably unsuccessful (the Canal blocked for the first time since it had been built and the Anglo/French forces replaced by United Nations troops after an unprecedented crisis in Anglo/American relations), Suez was a watershed in the decline of Britain as a world power, not only in the Middle East.

Nevertheless some moves in the old game of British influence could still be made. In 1958 there had been a civil war in Lebanon (the Iraqi units which carried out the coup in Baghdad had been en route to Lebanon to reinforce the embattled government) and American marines had landed on the Beirut beaches. Simultaneously British paratroops had landed in Jordan to protect – successfully as it turned out – King Hussein from suffering the fate of his cousin in Baghdad. Their job done, the British troops quietly withdrew a few months later.

Another major development since I had left Iraq in 1954 was the advent into the Middle East of the Soviet Union. Five years previously the Russians had nothing but an unimportant diplomatic presence in some, not all, Arab capitals. By 1959, the Soviet Union was building the Aswan High Dam (after Britain and the United States had withdrawn from the project) and was the principal supplier of military equipment to the United Arab Republic (after the Americans had turned down Egyptian requests for arms in 1955) and to revolutionary Iraq. The Russians were now major players in the Middle East game and the superpower confrontation had extended to the Levant: the old European powers had been relegated to a minor and still declining role. Even in Jordan, created and nurtured for so long by Britain, the Americans had assumed the lead both in financial and military support.

However, the aura of Britain as an imperial patron still hung over Amman and its environs. King Hussein had demonstrated his political, if not financial, independence three years before by sacking at a moment's notice the British commander of the Jordan Arab Army, Glubb Pasha, and by replacing all the British officers by Jordanians. But there were still British military training teams in the country and the King's personal pilot was a Scotsman from the Royal Air Force. The military establishments reeked of their recent British connexion and the West Bank Palestinians in particular regarded Whitehall, not Washington, as the power behind the throne. This belief was enhanced by such anachronisms as the fact that the British Ambassador and the Counsellor of the Embassy still occupied houses within the Palace compound where the King and his closest family lived and worked.

We were not popular: there was no doubt about that. Some of the more old-fashioned East Bank grandees clung to their British friends, but the younger, educated generation could not forgive us for having created the Palestine problem, for Suez, and, as they saw it, for abetting the Hashemite regime in obstructing the tide of republican Arab nationalism which, as they hoped, would lead to a wider Arab political unity. In so far as the government allowed public manifestations, they were more often than not directed against our Embassy, and I remember a good proportion of the information material which we distributed to 'opinion shapers' being returned in plain envelopes having first been torn to shreds.

Physically Jordan, East and West Banks, had altered little since my ignominious departure a decade earlier with the British retreat from Palestine. War and poverty had inhibited economic development. Only Aqaba, until recently no more than a fishing village at the head of the Red Sea, was beginning to exhibit signs of change. A new port was opened there in 1959 and a metalled road from the capital would shortly reduce the journey there from the leisurely but uncomfortable two days of the past to a few rapid hours.

Amman itself was a small, unpretentious garrison and market town climbing up the hills above a series of little valleys, while Arab Jerusalem had yet to develop the repulsive sprawl of Eastern European suburbs which have followed the Israeli occupation of 1967. The whole country had a bucolic, old-fashioned air, small towns serving the agricultural economy of small villages in the stony hills.

But the idyll ended with the outward appearance. Jordan was in the grip of a neurosis which was restrained only by the stern authority of the Jordanian Arab Army whose strong loyalty had maintained King Hussein on his throne through the turbulent vicissitudes of seven years. He had faced down plots, minor mutinies and determined attempts by the Egyptian regime to overthrow him, with skill and courage: always the devotion of the Bedouin units of the Army had proved the ultimate line of defence. On the East

Bank, the old Transjordan, the traditional acceptance of the Hashemite monarchy had been diluted by the massive influx of Palestinian refugees from the first Arab/Israeli wars of 1948-9. The West Bankers, apparently oblivious of the fact that, had it not been for the Arab Legion, they would have been swallowed by Israel at the outset, smouldered in resentment at Hashemite military rule and considered themselves as second-class citizens under an alien dispensation. Their longing to unite with the Union of Egypt and Syria was undisguised and their determination to break free was tempered only by the sure knowledge that an overt uprising would, if not firmly suppressed, almost certainly precipitate an Israeli invasion: it was generally accepted by even the most radical dissidents that Tel Aviv would not tolerate encirclement by a militantly hostile United Arab Republic stretching all the way from Damascus to Cairo.

Against this unpromising background, it would be reasonable to assume that the day-to-day conduct of relations between Britain, of all countries, and Jordan would be not only difficult but disagreeable. Not so. The long habit of political and personal intimacy with the British, dating back to the Arab Revolt of 1916, had descended to the present generation of leadership, and the Ambassador's relationship with the King and his government could not have been closer or easier. This was of course as it should be, in view of the shared interests of both countries. But even at my level, where I was in daily contact with Jordanians and Palestinians outside the governmental establishment, in many cases with men and women who were implacably opposed both to the Hashemite monarchy and to 'the British', I encountered no personal hostility. There is an important characteristic in which, in my opinion, Arabs emerge superior to Europeans. However deeply held their political convictions, they are capable of a total separation between their political and personal emotions which is far less common in Europe. In the case of the Palestinians, they had every reason to blame and to hate Britain for the loss of their land and the frustration of their aspiration to the self-determination which had come to virtually all the Arab successor states and peoples of the Ottoman Empire. The remark made by the Arab journalist, with which I opened this chapter, was not made frivolously or in jest. But our long association had bred a kind of empathy at a personal level. We laughed at the same jokes: we found the same things either ridiculous and distasteful or worthy of respect and admiration. We enjoyed the same kind of conversations. In short we liked each other as individuals beyond the superficialities of conventional politeness. Hence, although argument was invariably vigorous and uninhibited and the subject matter explosive, it was freed from mutual embarrassment or offence by this underlying element of personal goodwill.

At this point I can hear some of my readers saying to themselves: 'Ah, the archetypal Foreign Office Arabist has revealed himself. These people are blinded by the Lawrence myth and see themselves as latter-day men of the desert, trotting about on camels and living in black tents. No wonder their judgement is so suspect.' No, I am not writing of that kind of Anglo-Arab relationship, deep rooted though it was in the accounts of the nineteenth-century British travellers in the Arabian peninsula. I am an urban man and my Arab friends and acquaintances have been urban men, living and working in towns and cities – no hidden music of desert romance. If there is anything narcissistic in what I have written, it may be that I have read too much into the code of politeness to guests and strangers which is unquestionably part of the tradition of all Arabs, whether from the desert or from a great city. Perhaps I have mistaken civility for friendship. I still like to think not.

I admit that I had one significant advantage in my travels on the West Bank of Jordan twenty-five years ago. My daughter was at the time four years old and she and my wife used to accompany me as a matter of course. I can imagine the embarrassment and irritation which would be caused if a foreign diplomat in Britain were to arrive in his official capacity to call on, say, newspaper editors, university staff or local government dignitaries accompanied by an unannounced wife and a child. But my female entourage in Jordan was a great asset. Arabs love children – objective fact, not illusion – and our arrival with a small, red-haired and extremely friendly little girl immediately transformed the atmosphere and turned official calls into family occasions. Even when there was serious business to be discussed, my hosts, whether they were bemedalled Transjordanian generals, fiery journalists or radical Palestinian mayors, would not allow my family to go away and amuse themselves while the business part of the call was concluded. They would insist on my daughter remaining and participating in the discussion when they were not stuffing her with sweets, nuts and fruit. There is no doubt that bachelor diplomats and travellers in the Middle East are at a serious disadvantage vis-à-vis their more domesticated counterparts. In this context I remember driving one weekend from Amman to Beirut. We had to pass through Syria (at the time the Northern Province of the United Arab Republic, with which we had no diplomatic or consular relations). I was having considerable difficulty at the frontier with a group of surly and bureaucratic Syrian officials. It was night time and we were all tired and irritated. My daughter, who had been sleeping in the back of the car, suddenly reared up and asked what was going on. As soon as the Syrians saw her, their faces cleared. After exchanging some badinage with her in broken English, they stamped our passports without further delay and waved us goodbye as friends.

The Hashemite Kingdom of Jordan lacked the Gilbertian qualities which had made its sister kingdom in Iraq so attractive to those with a keen appreciation of the absurd. There was no Royal Harithiya Hunt in Amman, no Alwiya and Railway Clubs, indeed only a very small British community. There was no money to attract shoals of foreign businessmen and experts. Everything was on a smaller scale and the unpretentious style of the Royal Family and the political leadership contrasted pleasantly with the buffooneries of Hashemite Iraq. Not that they disseminated an atmosphere of puritanical austerity. Like their Iraqi counterparts, the Jordanians were genial people, not averse to the forbidden pleasures of Scotch whisky. The King enjoyed fast cars, go-karting, flying aeroplanes, the pastimes of a vigorous young graduate of Harrow and Sandhurst.

But business and pleasure were conducted with an absence of Ruritanian pomp and bombast. The senior and middle ranks of the officer corps had seen much action, not to speak of the rank and file, and there was little or no empty boasting to be heard.

In so far as the style of government owed anything to an infusion of foreign influence, it represented perhaps the best qualities of a British legacy. Transjordan had been a British Mandate for a good deal longer than Iraq, but the British presence had always been small, comprising a handful of officials who had devoted themselves to Jordan as it was rather than trying to transmute it into an imitation of the United Kingdom. The King, his family and some of the younger officials had benefited from British civilian and military education without losing an iota of their Arab identity. King Hussein was very much an Arab leader who had inculcated some of the best qualities taught at Harrow and Sandhurst. King Faisal II had been a young Englishman trying uneasily and reluctantly to resume an unfamiliar Arab guise. There was no gulf between ruler and people except in regard to the political desiderata of the Palestinian majority.

A British public school and the Royal Military College are admirable training grounds for the practice of benevolent dictatorship. There is no nonsense about democracy at these institutions. Boys at all levels are allowed a limited degree of participation in the administration of the school or college and are encouraged to take responsibility within a carefully defined framework. But the chain of command is absolute and owes nothing to electoral processes. Within the hierarchy each stratum is conscious of what is owed to the next above and by the next below, and there is no question as to who is the ultimate boss. So long as there is conformity and obedience throughout the structure and so long as the commander is conscious of his obligations as well as his privileges, the system works well enough. It can even, as in certain public schools, accommodate bogus elections to a bogus parliament, giving the inmates the illusion that they are playing a genuine part in the affairs of their little body politic.

Government in Jordan had evolved on lines similar to

these. Despite the sporadic and pro forma attempts by British advisers to persuade successive Hashemite rulers to democratise their political system, Kings Abdullah, Talal and Hussein had wisely resisted the temptation to adopt the Westminster model. The King ruled as well as reigned and, as with all the Arab successor states of the Ottoman Empire, he depended for his survival on the loyalty of his Armed Forces. But he could not have retained this loyalty if he had not demonstrated the qualities expected of a monarch – courage, skill, leadership and a sense of obligation towards those who supported him. King Hussein, for all his youthful impetuosity and inexperience, had already demonstrated his possession of these characteristics. His civilian advisers (Cabinet Ministers and the like) were mainly elderly and cautious East Bankers of proven loyalty and there were many competent technocrats, mainly Palestinians, further down the line of command.

As in Hashemite Iraq, there was a parliamentary system, scarcely more serious but less of a pretentious mockery. I used to attend sessions of the parliament, watching from the Diplomatic Box. The building was small, intimate, on a miniature scale: there cannot have been more than about 130 members. Debates were, like school debates, lively but limited in scope; even the most anti-Hashemite Palestinians knew better than publicly to traduce the state or the monarchy. Unreality hung in the air and everyone was conscious that the real action was going on elsewhere – on Cairo Radio, in the refugee camps, amongst West Bank plotters and exiles in Egypt and Syria, in the officers' messes, in the recesses of the Egyptian Intelligence Service.

In early 1960 I was transferred to Cairo. In 1958 I had been earmarked to open the Consulate-General (as it would have been) in Damascus, in the Northern Province of the United Arab Republic. But the prospect of the resumption of relations with the U.A.R. after the Suez break started to fade into the distance and I was sent, more or less as a temporary posting, to Amman. By the end of 1959 negotiations between Britain and Egypt for a resumption of relations were beginning to make progress and we had been allowed to establish a small Trade Mission, subsequently promoted to a Diplomatic Mission, in Cairo. Damascus still hung fire so I was eventually sent off to Cairo to act as Press Officer and First Secretary in the small Chancery there.

I welcomed this move: indeed I had on more than one occasion asked the Foreign Office for it. Not that I was unhappy in Jordan. Far from it. But I had long been convinced that Nasser's Egypt represented the tide of the future in the Arab world and that the kings, shaikhs, sultans and amirs would have to give place to this powerful, inspirational, unifying force. I believed that the best interests of Britain lay in catching this tide, not in attempting to turn it back as we had by setting up Hashemite Iraq as a challenge to Egypt (what futility) and finally by launching the disreputable fiasco of Suez. I thought that, if we played our cards with skill and sympathy, it would be possible for Britain to create a fresh and equal relationship with the renascent Arab world, unburdened by the imperialist impedimenta of the past.

During my short stay in Jordan I had experienced the palpable influence which Nasser's activities exercised over the political climate. Few people read the Jordanian newspapers except for local news and anti-Hashemite comment. Everyone read the Cairo newspapers (except when they were banned) as their main source of information and political guidance, just as they listened to Cairo Radio and the Cairo-based Voice of the Arabs (there was no television in the Arab world in those days). Cairo was the centre of the Jordanian universe and, love him or hate him, Nasser was the man who made Cairo's heartbeat audible from the Atlantic to the Persian Gulf. I remember a time when Nasser was visiting Damascus on a routine occasion. He delivered the usual clutch of speeches and press conferences. But his presence only a hundred miles or so from Amman created an atmosphere of such emotional excitement that, wherever I went, on the East or West Bank of Jordan, it seemed as if he were in the next room. It was as though a powerful electric current had been passed through the country. Such was his power over people's minds in those days.

And now I would be able to observe this phenomenon at first hand and perhaps play a microscopic part in repairing the damage done by Sir Anthony Eden's foolish adventure over three years previously. My wife and I had high hopes for the future but low expectations for the survival of the Hashemite regime in Jordan. I recall making a double bet with a Jordanian friend of mine, later assassinated by Palestinian terrorists. I bet him £200 that King Hussein would not last another two years. He bet me £200 that the United Arab Republic would have disintegrated within two years and that King Hussein would still be on the throne of Jordan. We played a drawn game, but the moral victory was his. King Hussein certainly survived; the United Arab Republic disintegrated two years and three or four months after our bet was laid.

We left Amman early in 1960. Those were still the days – the last days – of leisurely travel: there was no compulsion to take the fastest jet aircraft to cover the shortest distance between two points. We despatched our heavy luggage in advance and packed as much as we could into our Morris 1000 station wagon, a relic of our Ankara days. After a comfortable drive to Beirut, stopping en route for a final picnic at the enchanting Roman town of Jerash south of the frontier between Jordan and Syria, we embarked on one of the small but luxurious Italian passenger ships which operated throughout the eastern Mediterranean. A day or two later the ship drew into the harbour at Alexandria and we disembarked for the drive to Cairo. Another chapter in the story of our lives was about to open.

Twenty-five years later

If, on leaving Jordan in early 1960, I had been asked to forecast the outlines of the political situation in the Middle East in twenty-five years' time, I think I would have predicted a pattern of republican states dominated by a Nasserite Egypt, some of them in a more or less loose form of union with powerful neighbours, for example Egypt, Syria or Iraq, depending on the facts of geography, with the Arab/Israeli conflict still raging and East/West competition constituting a driving force in the foreign, economic and defence procurement policies of the regional states. I would probably have gone on to speculate that Turkey and Iran would remain stable and pro-Western, thus to some extent insulating the Arab World from the worst dangers of the Cold War. I would have anticipated the withdrawal of the remainder of the British imperial presence from the Arabian peninsula and, with the adoption of sensible policies (there were already some signs of grace emerging from London in the aftermath of Suez), the establishment of a normal relationship between Britain and the Arabs, a relationship based on mutual interest, not on the inequalities of the past. Had I adumbrated such a sketch of the future, there would have been many people, both Arab and British, who would have agreed with me.

Now, let us say that I had suggested something quite different. Let us say that I had spoken as follows. In twenty-five years' time, Egypt will be capitalist, pro-Western, at peace with and in treaty relations with Israel. The monarchical and traditional regimes of the Arabian peninsula will be stronger than ever: even following the withdrawal of British protection, the same shaikhs and amirs of the Persian Gulf will still be ruling their states, which will all be independent members of the Arab League and the United Nations. The Shah will have fallen to a mass revolution which will have brought a medieval theocrat to power in Iran. War between Iran and Iraq will have been going on for five years in the general area of the southern oilfields, but without the Great Powers having become involved. The Lebanese state will have collapsed in civil war and anarchy. Israel will have been in occupation of the West Bank of Jordan, the Gaza Strip and the Golan Heights for eighteen years and will have become a bristling garrison state dependent almost entirely on the United States of America. European influence will have declined to negligible proportions but the United States, notwithstanding its overt championship of Israel, will be courted by most Arab states for its economic power and potential ability to bring pressure on its Israeli protégé: the Soviet Union will have been pushed to the sidelines, retaining a precarious foothold only in Syria and in the unimportant, albeit Communist, People's Democratic Republic of the Yemen, the successor state to the

Colony of Aden and the Aden Protectorates. Above all the Hashemite monarchy in Jordan will have survived: King Hussein will be regarded as one of the elder statesmen of the Arab world, his internal position and external influence stronger than at any time in his long reign. Had I spoken on these lines in 1960, there would I believe have been a disposition to consign me to a lunatic asylum. And yet, all this is exactly what has happened.

How wrong some of us were all those years ago, although for a time it looked as though we would be proved right. Throughout the early and mid-1960s the pressure grew against the Arab kings, particularly King Hussein, and, notwithstanding the disintegration of the union between Egypt and Syria in 1961, the Nasserist vision of Arab nationalism seemed bound eventually to prevail. The June war of 1967 changed everything. I have described the dramatic events leading up to that disaster for Arab arms and its consequences in Chapter Five on Bahrain and will not anticipate that account here. Jordan was caught up in the tempest of Arab excitement which followed Nasser's reoccupation of Sinai and the expulsion of the United Nations Emergency Force in May 1967, and King Hussein felt obliged not only to form a common military front with Egypt but also to attack across the cease-fire lines on the 6th of June. As a result Jordan lost Arab Jerusalem and the West Bank to Israel's armies, which were quick to take advantage of such an opportunity.

During the following three years, the fate of the Jordanian monarchy hung in the balance, although the dynamic of Nasserism had suffered a mortal blow from the catastrophe of June 1967. A fresh threat arose from the emergence of a militant Palestinian consciousness under the banner of the Palestine Liberation Organisation. From 1948 until 1967 the Palestinian Arabs had been content to leave their destiny in the hands of the Arab League and its leader, Egypt. After the June war, they decided to take matters into their own hands and the P.L.O. developed from being an obscure guerrilla organisation with a Cairo-controlled political wing, into what quickly amounted to a state within a state, seeking and, to a large extent, obtaining world-wide recognition as

45

the authentic voice of Palestinian nationalism. Naturally enough the P.L.O. chose Jordan as their initial base for operations and, by 1970, King Hussein was in danger of ceasing to be master in his own house. In September 1970, with characteristic resolution, he decided to have it out with the Palestinians who were defeated in bloody fighting in which Syria briefly and unsuccessfully joined. The P.L.O. moved their operation to southern Lebanon, and unchallenged Hashemite authority was restored in Jordan. A few months later, in 1971, I visited Amman.

I had flown in from Cairo, a scene of defeat and depression. Morale in Egypt was low: the towns along the Suez Canal had been destroyed in the war of attrition which followed the 1967 conflict and the city was thronged with disaffected and miserable refugees. It was raining and the piles of torn sandbags at the entrances to government buildings were vomiting mud on to the cracked pavements. The shops were empty of goods and the large hotels half-deserted. My old friends were as charming and amusing as ever, but it was not difficult to sense their underlying despair.

The contrast with Amman was unbelievable. Here everything was fresh and clean in the bright Jordanian autumn; the people were active and prosperous: against all the odds the city was booming. The old question of how Jordan could exist without Anglo-American financial subsidies sounded like a voice from a long-buried past. Arab money had poured into the country since the 1967 war, while the preliminary tremors of the civil war which was shortly to engulf the Lebanon had brought even more wealth to Jordan. The property market was thriving and the city stretched far beyond the limits which I had known a dozen years previously. The tension which had gripped Jordan since the June war had broken with the expulsion of the P.L.O., and the country seemed more at peace with itself than at any time I had known it since 1948.

Today, the contrast with Jordan of twenty-five years ago is infinitely more profound. My wife and I visit the country in April, 1985. We land at a new, and by international standards, attractive airport some twenty miles south of

Amman and are driven quickly into the city along a wide highway. And it is a city. The rolling hills where we used to take country walks and picnics in the past are covered with square, stone houses, stretching to the horizon. The population of Amman, perhaps 70,000 in our time, has grown to about one million. 'Where have all the people come from?' we ask. Apparently the natural rate of increase of Jordan's population is around 4 per cent a year, amongst the highest in the world. A trickle from the West Bank and the attraction of the capital for the countryside have done the rest. It is impossible to find the old landmarks: a new complex of office buildings stands where our old house used to be. And yet the essential nature of the place has not changed. There is no sign of the shanties and slums which are so familiar a feature of most rapidly developing capital cities. The market area is much larger and new shopping centres have sprouted to serve the many suburban centres which have come into existence. But there are few steel and glass tower blocks and other sacrifices to prestige. It is still a pleasant place, maintaining something of the atmosphere of middle-class rusticity which was always its characteristic.

Wherever we go the same transformations strike us. Jordan now has three universities – none in my day. The Jordan valley, a wasteland in the 1950s, is now a thriving and populous agricultural area. Electricity, piped water, schools and social services have reached deep into the countryside. Setting aside cultural differences, the basic standard of living is analogous to that of any country in the Eastern Mediterranean basin. There is much talk of retrenchment and recession but, to someone who knew the country in the 1940s and 1950s, these jeremiads seem slightly weird. Even to the most casual observer it is obvious that there is plenty of money about, especially in the private sector, and any retreat there may be will take place from an economic plateau of a height which would have been beyond the imagination of anyone who knew Jordan in the past.

Quite apart from the spectacular changes, there is today a sense of solidity, of genuine national cohesion in Jordan, which was absent a quarter of a century ago. This may appear a bold judgement after a visit of only a few days'

47

duration, but I had the advantage of being able to talk in complete freedom to many of my friends from the past, some, like myself, now retired, others occupying high positions in government, the academic world and the private sector. No one would question the debt owed by the country to the courage, experience and resourcefulness of the King and to the dynamic energy and creative power across the whole field of development activity of his brother the Crown Prince. Were it not for one apparently intractable question, the future for Jordan would be bright indeed, and the problems of a rapidly developing country easily manageable, given the present leadership and the deep reserves of national talent and dedication on which the King and his brother can draw.

But the dense cloud of Palestine looms over everything and everybody, and all conversations, wherever they may begin, soon come round to it. The atmosphere of frustration is palpable, particularly since the Jordanians are conscious on the Arab side of a greater readiness for peace than at any time in the past. Meanwhile, as the dispute festers, more Jordanians, particularly of the younger generation, are turning to Islamic militancy as the only cure for their ills and an alarming gap is growing between them and the rationality of their parents.

Here lies King Hussein's most obstinate dilemma. Jordan is now reconciled with Egypt and with Iraq; Syria remains the only significant Arab country which cherishes hostility to his policies. Even the leadership of the mainstream of the P.L.O. has come round. But all the King's efforts with his friends in the West, particularly the United States, have so far failed to generate the pressure necessary to induce Israel to disgorge those remaining parts of Mandatory Palestine which she seized in 1967. Meanwhile Israel has steadily absorbed these territories through the appropriation of land and water supplies and the establishment of over a hundred Jewish settlements. There will be no real peace for Jordan, or for Israel for that matter, until the consequences of the June War have been redeemed. And if frustration over the stalemate leads, as well it may, particularly in these days of the renascence of militant Islam, to the radicalisation of the

Arab world and the commitment of Arab states to a solution through armed struggle alone, the first country to feel the impact will be Jordan. The King, if he survives, will be forced to make a choice between sustaining moderate policies in co-operation with his friends in the West who have so far delivered so little over this central foreign and domestic policy issue for his country, and turning to more dangerous and fundamentalist paths in order to placate his people, perhaps in the company of more ruthless and cynical allies whose blandishments he has so far resisted. I have already indicated the difficulty in accurately predicting events in this part of the world. But this is one prediction of which I feel confident, even though the timing of its coming to pass cannot be foreseen. I believe that the time left to enable Jordan to avoid being faced with so grim a choice is fast running out. Once Israeli absorption of the West Bank is accepted as irreversible even by the most naive of optimists, then will it become impossible for Jordan any longer to justify to its people a policy of peaceful settlement, particularly if such a policy identifies the country with those outside powers, above all the United States, which all Arabs regard as being responsible for championing Israel in her expansionist rejection of all efforts to secure a negotiated peace.

For the time being the last redoubt of Sharif Hussein's Arab Revolt against the Ottoman Empire seventy years ago continues to hold out. For the Sharif the 'stars' bridle was hung too high'. His vision of an independent and united Arab kingdom ruled from Mecca faded when Britain, setting European considerations above her wartime commitments to the Arabs, did nothing to prevent France from sweeping Prince Faisal from his newly established seat in Damascus in 1920. Four years later the old Sharif himself was in exile and his son, Ali, had been ejected from the Sharifian heartland of the Hijaz by the forces of Abdul Aziz Ibn Saud. Nevertheless Hashemite kings ruled the Levant Arab world from the borders of Iran to the frontiers where Palestine/Israel meet with Syria until the coup d'état in Baghdad destroyed the throne and took the life of Sharif Hussein's great-grandson, Faisal II, in 1958. Now, only his other great-grandson, Hussein, remains ruling a small kingdom fortuitously carved out of the original boundaries of Mandatory Palestine to accommodate his grandfather Abdullah, following the deposition by France of Prince Faisal, a kingdom the existence of which no one connected with the original Arab Revolt had envisaged.

In practice it has proved the most durable of all the Arab regimes which emerged from the debris of the Ottoman Empire in the period immediately following the end of the First World War. No one would have predicted such a consummation, namely that the economically unviable, socially divided and politically explosive kingdom inherited by King Hussein in 1952 would outlast the monarchies of Iraq and Libya, the Venetian-style republic of Lebanon, the imperial throne of Iran and, last but not least, the pan-Arab dream of the King's arch-antagonist, President Nasser of Egypt. Britain helped in the early days with financial and military support and with development aid. The United States contribution had, by the close of the 1950s, exceeded that of Britain, and America today is Jordan's senior partner outside the region. Even so Britain and Jordan remain close and intimate friends at all levels. Much abides in Jordan as a legacy of the British connexion and King Hussein is held in admiring affection by the people of Britain to a greater extent than any other Middle East leader. And so he should be. It has been his courage, his skill, his experience and his leadership which have done more than anything or anyone else to hold his country together over more than thirty years of political crisis and intermittent warfare. Those of us, like myself, who have known Jordan for more than half of its lifetime, will always wish the country well.

THREE

Egypt

My wife and I and our four-year-old daughter stared at the advancing outline of the city of Alexandria as our comfortable, even sybaritic, Italian passenger ship approached the harbour in early 1960. The façade of buildings on the long seafront looked much the same as it had looked from the deck of the military vessel on which I had sailed for the Italian campaign in 1943, seventeen years previously. The disorderly, shouting confusion of the dockside made my departure seem like yesterday and, as we disembarked, the demands for baksheesh were no less vocal or pressing. Revolution and the advent of Arab socialism had not, at first sight, made much difference to the noisy, good-humoured, genial people of Egypt.

Delay in landing our car and luggage meant that we had to stay overnight in Alexandria before driving to Cairo. As we entered the city I received my first shock. When I had briefly and superficially known it years before, Alexandria had been the Alexandria of Lawrence Durrell's books. Vital, cosmopolitan, the very rich and very poor struggling for passage on the pavements, it had flaunted the colour and vivacity which had no doubt characterised it for centuries, if not millennia. Now it was a dying city. The Cecil Hotel, where we stayed, was a mausoleum of empty rooms, more staff than guests, and the streets and shops had the same atmosphere of crumbling, moribund decay. The houses of the rich, shuttered in overgrown walled gardens, looked uninhabited, abandoned. What had happened? Obviously the pashas must have been reduced from their former opulence by Nasser's egalitarian policies. By the same token many of the cosmopolitan minorities, particularly the Greeks, must have upped sticks and departed. But where

51

was the dynamic energy that, we had been told, had been released by the revolution of 1952 and its liberating measures? It would be some months before I found answers to these questions. For the time being the degenerate condition of this once great city provided an intriguing conundrum, particularly to someone who had returned to Egypt in the most favourable frame of mind towards the new dispensation.

Our little Morris 1000 station wagon, veteran of Turkey and Jordan, rushed along the desert road from Alexandria to Cairo. Here again there were novelties, this time to be expected. Gone were the streams of British camouflaged military vehicles which used to dominate the handful of battered taxis and the limousines of the rich. In their place, military vehicles of a different kind, comparable in numbers, but unfamiliar, heavy, archaic – the fruits of Soviet military assistance. Away to the west, where only sand had drifted before, there were signs of orderly cultivation, ploughing, irrigation ditches, sprinklers, small settlements: this must be the famous Liberation Province, an embryonic attempt by the government to provide more room for the peasants of the overcrowded Nile Valley. Close to the Pyramids, a new military airfield came in sight: again the aircraft circling overhead looked unfamiliar – Russian-made fighters and transport planes.

Cairo at last. We drove along the new corniche on the East bank of the Nile, the road which had trimmed a few yards off the British Embassy garden, which had previously stretched to the edge of the river. Close to the Embassy, a block of tall flats had been built and a new, not unattractive, Shepheard's Hotel had replaced the famous hotel of that name in the centre of the city. Our destination was next door, the old Semiramis, a fleeting memory of mine from wartime days. The lavish staff of elderly and friendly Nubians, as always dressed in white galabiyyehs with red tarbooshes on their heads, welcomed us and decanted us in a vast, Victorian double bedroom, complete with a bathroom of 'nineties style and vintage, plus a small bed in the corner for our daughter. It was early afternoon and we were ready to start.

The Semiramis was our home for the next six weeks while we looked for a furnished flat or house. This was a new experience for us in the Arab world. In my bachelor days I had lived in tents, barracks or police posts. In Baghdad and Amman we had taken over the houses occupied by our predecessors. Only in Ankara had we undergone the grim torment of househunting from the base of a second-rate Middle Eastern hotel. It had not been an experience which encouraged repetition. With their strong sense of superiority and national pride, the Turks, at least in those days, must have been among the worst hoteliers in the world. Our rooms had been dingy, ill-fitted and depressing. Even breakfast, let alone any other meals, had been unobtainable. The presence of a large black rat discouraged use of the bathroom. The staff, if they could be called by so pretentious a name, were surly and offhand: simple requests, politely framed, were regarded as arrogant demands for impossible favours and responded to accordingly. The living accommodation for which we were so diligently searching, spurred on by our intense longing to escape from the Park Palace Oteli and the string of third-rate restaurants around which my wife, then pregnant with our daughter, myself and our two small boys used to trail dejectedly three times a day, was overpriced and reminiscent of what I imagined to be the flats of middle-rank party officials in an Eastern European capital. It was only when, after about two months of this constant violation of our basic human rights, I blackmailed my immediate boss in the Embassy by threatening to return to London with my family if he did not authorise me to accept the next badly furnished, over-priced – but just adequate – apartment which we saw, that the moment of deliverance arrived.

With these memories still vivid in our minds, even after the passage of over five years, we set out from the Semiramis on the househunting trail with heavy hearts. We were also mildly apprehensive of the reception we might meet from the Egyptian landlords and families whose houses and flats we would be examining. Only three years previously British troops had invaded their country, British aircraft had bombed their airfields, in collusion with their deadly enemy who had simultaneously occupied most of that part of Egypt lying east of the Suez Canal: significant casualties, both in lives and property, had been sustained by the Egyptians: diplomatic relations had been severed and British property in Egypt seized.

I was also conscious that the seventy years of British domination of Egypt from 1882 until the Young Officers Revolution of 1952, had not endeared us to the middle-class, educated Egyptians of the kind whose houses we would be seeking to rent for ourselves. 'The British' had long been the bogeymen of Egyptian folklore, the 'hidden hand' behind Egyptian politics and policies, the puppeteers pulling the strings of Egyptian financial, economic, educational, agricultural and all other aspects of policy and development. The British Embassy was well known to have been the third pillar in a pyramid of power which had to be taken into account when any change was mooted – the other two being the Palace and the principal political parties. The cosmopolitan pashas and beys, Turks, Armenians, Circassians, Syrians, who had thrived on this system and adapted themselves happily to regarding the British as a welcome part of their constellation of political and social intrigue, had been dispossessed and we were now face to face with those Egyptians who had traditionally regarded us with resentment.

Over twenty years later I asked an Egyptian friend of mine why it was that his countrymen used to dislike us so much. We had after all been more directly imperialistic over an even longer period in the small states of the Persian Gulf: we had been the creators of the Palestine problem. And yet I had not been aware of a generalised aversion to the British in these other parts of the Arab world. On the contrary, for all our political differences, it was undeniable that many Englishmen were regarded with genuine respect and affection.

'Yes,' my friend replied. 'You sent some admirable Englishmen to the remoter parts of the Arab world. They were loved for themselves and were identified as "our" Englishmen as distinct from the "British". Not so in Egypt. You despised the Egyptians and it showed. The French did not and we appreciated them. We had "our" Frenchmen. But Lord Cromer, Lord Kitchener and the earlier generation of British officials, although they undoubtedly laid the foundations of modern Egypt, were cold and aloof – with some notable exceptions. Perhaps you did not like us because we were too sophisticated. We confronted you with ideas and intellectual opposition. We made you feel uncomfortable and you reacted by characterising us as devious Levantines, too clever by half.'

Certainly, my friend's analysis is reflected in the memoirs of Egyptian nationalists writing about their feelings towards Britain in the first half of this century. T. E. Lawrence sensed the atmosphere. 'None the less, the Egyptian townsmen do hate us so. I thought it was only a coldness ... but it is a most burning dislike,' he wrote in a letter from the Grand Continental Hotel in Cairo dated 2nd February 1915. At an earthier level, the late President Sadat, in his autobiography *In Search of Identity*, wrote that, as a child in an Egyptian village, he had learned to hate the British. He tells a story of how the villagers admired Napoleon for allegedly defying the British Governor of St Helena. 'This was obviously an old wives' tale, but it reflected a living concept of heroism in the Egyptian mind, particularly as their hero was a powerful enemy of the British – our enemies, the people who occupied our land and whose presence was resisted in every possible way.'

To return to our househunting. In those few weeks we must have met a wider cross-section of Egyptians and their families than we would have in months of assiduous diplomatic cultivation. In spite of the unpromising portents, we warmed immediately to them. We were greeted with invariable courtesy and there was never a question of our viewing a house without being pressed to accept hospitality. We found ourselves amongst good-humoured, easy-going, intelligent people. With great tact the subject of the Suez invasion was gently side-stepped: there were many expressions of welcome for our return to Egypt after what was described as 'an unfortunate episode' in our relationship. Conversation took place sometimes in Arabic, sometimes in English but most often in French, a testament to the deep cultural influence of France in the century and a half since Napoleon's brief occupation of the country. As was the case elsewhere in the Arab world, the presence of my small daughter was an unqualified asset. On a similar search in Britain she would have been an equally unqualified liability. My wife used to explain to our potential landlords and landladies that we did have three rather lively children, her mind running on the possible fate of the ornaments and elaborate furnishings of many of the houses which we saw. She was invariably misunderstood. She would be asked what the problem was. There was plenty of room for the children and they would enjoy playing in the garden. What was worrying her? Why did she make special mention of the children as if they were some kind of threat? On only one occasion did we encounter the reaction we would have expected in our own country. When my wife, as usual, confessed to having three children, one Egyptian house-owner said with obvious shame that his wife had insisted that they let their flat only to a childless couple. Such was his discomfort at what was clearly to him an incomprehensible restriction, that he eventually felt obliged to admit that his wife was English.

We finally found what we wanted, a large flat in the central suburb of Zamalek overlooking the Aquarium Gardens. We left the Semiramis, of which my daughter had by that time become a kind of unofficial manageress, with a twinge of regret and settled in.

The team which I had joined was one of the smallest and happiest of my career in diplomacy. The founder members had arrived in Cairo some months earlier to begin the arduous, but absorbing, task of restoring relations with the United Arab Republic. When I arrived, the British Trade Mission, as it had originally been called, had just been promoted to the status of a Diplomatic Mission – an exchange of Ambassadors was still over a year away in the future – and we had been allowed to resume occupation of the Embassy building which had been constructed to accommodate a staff of more than ten times the size of our handful of diplomats, secretaries, clerks and security guards. None of us was tainted in Egyptian eyes by previous service in Cairo in the old days of 'British imperialism', and we were fortunate to be led by that nicest and most sensitive of men, Colin Crowe, an inspired choice to be the first Chargé d'Affaires.

There was plenty to do, much of it of a complex and delicate nature. The Egyptian authorities, although personally friendly enough, were justifiably suspicious and politically cautious – they could not be seen to be falling over themselves to effect a reconciliation with a country which had only recently been a leading participant in the 'Tripartite Aggression', as the Suez affair was known. They did not go out of their way to make things easy for us and, apart from the principal negotiation about a gradual restoration of full relations, there were plenty of associated subjects to occupy us: the reopening of British consular posts, the desequestration of British property, the resumption of trade and so on, all of which required reciprocal concessions to Egypt.

My own job, working to Geoffrey Arthur, the Political Counsellor, and to Colin Crowe, was not narrowly defined. I was to keep a general eye on the Egyptian political situation and on the foreign policy of the United Arab Republic, to study the Egyptian press and the other public information media and to act as Press Officer with the swarm of British and other foreign journalists who were either resident in Cairo or frequent visitors from Beirut. Geoffrey Arthur who, with Colin, became my lifelong friend, was also an inspired choice. With wide experience of the Middle East and a first-class command of classical and modern Arabic, he was one of the most intelligent men I had ever met. I was lucky to have the chance to work with two such outstanding colleagues, both of whom rose high in the Service: Colin Crowe ending his career over ten years later as British Ambassador to the United Nations and Geoffrey Arthur becoming the last Political Resident in the Persian Gulf before retiring to be Master of Pembroke College, Oxford, where he suddenly died in 1984, to me and his many friends an irreparable loss. Looking back over twenty-five years, I suppose that the three of us had, amongst many other things, one important feature in common: we were basically sympathetic to the aspirations of the regime in Egypt and correspondingly determined to do what little we could to erase the memories of the past and to create a fresh and equal relationship between Britain and the U.A.R. We saw no prima-facie reason, for all the external evidence, why our two countries should be perpetual adversaries. I addressed myself dutifully to the study of the Cairo press and radio. The regime itself was secretive and inaccessible, particularly to us British, and part of my task was to deduce from a careful analysis of the newspapers what was really going on. The newspapers were closely controlled by the government, a situation which was regularised shortly after my arrival by nationalisation, and a military censor sat in every editorial office. The press was in fact regarded more as a vehicle for 'national guidance' than a medium for the communication of information and pluralistic comment. We had virtually no locally engaged staff and my first duty every day was to read all the newspapers and periodicals from cover to cover. This was not only good for my Arabic but not as arduous as it sounds: although deadly boring after a time. They were all printing almost identical news and comment. The external radio channels were more fun. The Voice of the Arabs poured out an endless stream of vituperation directed against the current targets of the regime. Zionism and imperialism led the field but those Arab governments which had failed to espouse the Nasserist cause had a hard time of it, particularly Saudi Arabia and the Hashemite Kingdom of Jordan. 'Stooge' and 'hireling' were two of the mildest but most frequent characterisations. 'The British' still came in for their fair share, particularly on account of our continuing presence in Aden and the Aden Protectorates, and more generally because of our apparently irredeemable imperialist propensities. Another radio station, 'The Voice of the Gulf', directed its fire at the traditional regimes in the small states of the Persian Gulf and their British protectors.

After a time I began to think I was seeing the picture with more clarity. The exhortations of the leadership and their reflections in press, radio and television assumed a discernible pattern. The regime was anti-capitalist, anticolonialist, anti-imperialist, anti-Zionist, anti-monarchist. By extension it was socialist, egalitarian, republican, pro-Arab unity on its terms, pro-liberation movements. In foreign policy the watchword was 'positive neutrality and non-alignment', a portmanteau slogan which in practice seemed to mean giving the Soviet Union the benefit of just about every doubt and the West the benefit of none (Nasser was, of course, with Nehru, Tito and Soekarno a founder member of the Non-Aligned Movement which was born out of the Bandoeng Conference of 1955).

What seemed lacking was the systematisation of the array of slogans into an articulated philosophy of government. The Young Officers had seized power eight years previously in order to slay a large number of dragons who without doubt had it coming to them. Every dragon slain left a gap in their programme. They reminded me of the Old Lady in the Babar books who, at the successful conclusion of another dangerous adventure, would gather the elephants round her and ask, 'Well, what shall we do now?'

This was particularly true of the structure of internal politics. The regime, Nasser included, did not wish to perpetuate naked military government. But all their efforts to broaden the political base had turned into farce. No one had taken the 'Liberation Rally' seriously and the sceptical Egyptians were now pouring scorn on the latest version, the 'National Union', later to become the 'Arab Socialist Union'. The National Union was constructed as a step pyramid of democracy with elected representatives at each level electing a smaller number of representatives to the next level. But without any clear political creed, such as Marxism/Leninism, or a multiplicity of political parties, as in a Western democracy, it degenerated into a sterile contest of personalities each trying to excel the other in egregious sycophancy towards the ruling officers, the objective being to propitiate them and thus to enable ordinary people to get on with their lives with the minimum of interference from central government.

The pathos of this quest for legitimacy was exemplified in Nasser's pamphlet 'The Philosophy of the Revolution'. I had heard of this work when I was in Jordan and bought a copy soon after my arrival in Cairo. I had expected a weighty book of some hundreds of pages. Instead I found myself the possessor of a booklet a few pages long. Being naturally suspicious I asked an Egyptian journalist friend of mine where I could obtain a copy of the true version. I could not believe that this short collection of generalisations and platitudes was the real thing. My copy must be either for children or for foreigners with limited knowledge of Arabic. No, my friend assured me, what I had was all there was to the philosophy of the revolution.

Perhaps the most distressing manifestation of Nasser's rule was the pervasiveness and, by the relatively mild standards of Egypt, ruthlessness of the secret police. Admittedly Nasser had experienced genuine problems, with the Communists and the fanatics of the Muslim Brotherhood, with Israeli agents and with discontent in parts of the Armed Forces at the time of the enforced resignation of General Naguib in 1954. But the ubiquity of the intelligence apparatus on which Nasser had come to depend had disseminated an atmosphere of fear which compounded the totalitarianism of a country with a controlled press and a parliamentary system which could scarcely be dignified even as a rubber stamp. Telephones were liberally tapped, conversations eavesdropped, and the Citadel was full of people who had allegedly offended against the state. Beatings and torture were by no means unknown.

Foreigners were not exempted from these unwelcome attentions. The tapping of our telephones and the exercise of pressure on our servants were blatant. We used to turn this to our advantage. When Egyptian officialdom obstructed the implementation of some concession to which the regime had agreed, we would resort to the transparent device of sending someone back to his flat and telephoning him from the Embassy. The speaker would complain loudly that such and such was not happening: we were sure that it would if only Gamal Abdul Nasser, who had so generously agreed in principle to our request, realised that a road-block had been erected lower down the bureaucratic line. As a rule this stratagem worked: sometimes the obstacle was cleared away the following day.

I also recall my poor old sufragi, who knew about twenty words of English, continuing to pour wine into a guest's glass at dinner in my flat until the whole bottle had been decanted over his trousers, so hard was he concentrating on the flow of English conversation which he obviously had to report on later in the evening. The doorman of our block of flats used to make such heavy weather of trying to identify all my guests that I eventually took pity on him and provided him with lists of their names in Arabic, as an ultimate gesture of goodwill. In this general respect, we were fortunate in having diplomatic immunity: the grotesque surveillance was more of a bad joke to us than a form of persecution. Other foreigners, notably journalists, were less favoured. It was not uncommon for foreign correspondents to return from an evening out to find that their flats had been ransacked, and the restrictions on filing copy became so exacting that many of them left the beating heart of the Arab world for the more relaxed atmosphere of Beirut.

How did the people of Cairo regard their rulers? Egypt is probably the oldest and most homogeneous nation state in the world and its people have developed a sophisticated and sceptical attitude towards government. In spite of the very real danger of incarceration and torture if they stepped out of line, their humorous and extrovert natures made them indiscreet to the point of foolhardiness. Even in public: some newspaper cartoonists used to sail very close to the censor's wind and I have little doubt that many of the most adulatory leading articles could be interpreted quite differently by discerning readers. My own friends and acquaintances used to talk to me with great frankness, even on the telephone, sometimes with serious results for them. It was, as I have suggested, very difficult to penetrate the inner counsels of the regime but it was less difficult to find out what the educated man in the street thought about them.

I did not mix with the handful of ci-devant aristocrats who still lived in Cairo. If I had I might have heard a different story. My circle of acquaintances included journalists, artists, academics, some businessmen, people like that. I never heard anyone lament the passing of the monarchy. Nasser was personally respected and admired, for his incorruptibility, his simple life style, his obvious good intentions towards his people. Above all he had given them self-respect and dignity by liberating the country from foreign domination and by establishing Egypt as the centre of the non-aligned world stage. My friends argued about specific policies – socialism and mass nationalisation – and they disliked the totalitarian flavour of the regime. But they welcomed the reduction in disparity between rich and poor, the distribution of land to previously sharecropping peasants, and the creation of opportunities for the emergent middle class. They were proudly conscious of the fact that Nasser and his colleagues, many of whom came in for their fair share of ribald humour and scandalous gossip, represented the first genuinely Egyptian government which the country had had for centuries.

An interesting phenomenon was the comparative lack of interest in pan-Arab adventurism. The Egyptians took it for granted that Cairo was the metropolis of Arab civilisation and culture. Egypt was the only country in the Arab world with an old established press and radio, a flourishing film industry, a considerable corpus of modern literature, international sporting prowess, etc., etc. The other Arab countries were merely rustic provinces. In spite of the propagandist ballyhoo about the United Arab Republic, I met no one who had bothered to visit the capital of the Syrian region, Damascus, and I recall the resentment of Egyptians at having to put 'Arabi' in the nationality box on passport forms instead of 'Misri' (Egyptian).

The general attitude towards the Palestine problem differed from that which I had experienced elsewhere in the Arab world. Naturally enough it obsessed the people of Jordan, the majority of whom were themselves Palestinians, and Iraq had espoused Palestine as an imperative of the foreign policy range of a new Arab nation establishing its identity. Notwithstanding the incessant stream of anti-Israeli, anti-Zionist and anti-Western (Israel's friends) propaganda which poured out of the Cairo press and radio, the Egyptians as a whole regarded Palestine more soberly. Although Israel was never formally acknowledged by name in the media – it was always the 'Zionist entity' or the 'usurping entity' – there was a noticeable tendency in conversation to regard the continuing war between Israel and Egypt rather as a quarrel between states, than an emotional and passionate issue concerning 'sacred soil'.

Egypt had fought Israel twice over the previous fourteen years and had paid a heavier price in casualties than any other Arab state. Egypt had occupied the Gaza Strip since 1948 and had used it as a base for launching guerrilla raids into Israeli territory: this had provoked savage retaliation. The Egyptian heartland had been threatened in 1956 by the tripartite assault of Israel, Britain and France, and the Egyptian province of Sinai was now demilitarised under the occupation of the first United Nations Emergency Force. There was no doubt that, even though the level of popular emotion in Cairo might be lower, Egypt was a country far more obviously mobilised for war, far more demonstrably in the front line, than Hashemite Iraq, or for that matter, the Syrian region of the U.A.R. Even the West Bank of Jordan gave a more tranquil impression of peacetime activity than did the heavily militarised Egyptian region of the Union. Nasser was certainly ready to carry on the fight and had made himself the standard-bearer of the Palestine cause throughout the Arab world. His people would follow his lead but without the fire and frenzy of the Jordanian refugee camps, of the bazaars of Amman and Damascus, the cafés of Beirut and Baghdad.

There was some genuine pride in Cairo's being the centre for national liberation movements, particularly from colonial territories in Africa. Not only was the Egyptian government host to the Afro-Asian Peoples Solidarity Organisation, a forcing bed of high-flown rhetoric with its fair share of bonhomous Soviet gentlemen with names like Ahmedov, but there was scarcely an African country which did not have an office in Cairo emitting streams of propaganda against its colonial rulers. Kenya, Uganda, Tanganyika, Zanzibar and the African National Congress come to mind. In the turbulent aftermath of the independence of the Belgian Congo, I remember asking a working-class Egyptian acquaintance of mine about the level of literacy in the

U.A.R. He replied that the problem had been solved: everyone could read. When I expressed mild wonder at this claim, he replied that, to be literate, it was necessary only to be able to read two words which appeared daily in banner headlines in every newspaper. They were 'Lumumba' and 'Imperialism'. Everyone could by now recognise them.

This predilection for African liberation caused occasional problems. After the murder of Prime Minister Lumumba of the Congo, a 'spontaneous' demonstration marched towards the Belgian Embassy, a few yards away from the British Embassy building. I was looking out of my office window and realised that some form of spontaneity was about to be manifested when camera teams from the state-owned television service began to set up shop in the empty street outside the Belgian Chancery. A handful of Egyptian police then arrived, sufficient in numbers to control the well-organised and biddable Egyptian crowd whom they were clearly expecting. Suddenly a mob of black Africans, students and exiles from the yet to be liberated African states, stormed up the street. A diversionary attack was mounted on our building, for form's sake, I imagined, and my ears rang to the sound of breaking glass. A number of us went down to the car park to push our cars out of the line of fire of flying stones, spurred on by the ribald encouragement of our friends from the foreign press corps who were covering the African demonstration from the other side of our fence. Having enjoyed themselves briefly at our expense, the Africans set about the Belgian Chancery in earnest. The police found themselves faced with men of sterner stuff than the docile Cairo crowds with whom they were accustomed to dealing, and the building was soon burning fiercely. I remember seeing the Ambassador and his staff jumping into the back garden from a first-floor window in order to escape the flames.

The Sharpeville massacre in 1960 enabled the regime to solve an intriguing dilemma. Notwithstanding the strident support for African liberation, there was still a South African Legation in Cairo when I first arrived. After Sharpeville, Nasser took a little time to decide what to do. For two or three days the incident was not mentioned in the Cairo

media. So far as the Egyptian public were concerned it had
not happened until the government had made up its mind
what line to take. In the event, the decision was taken to
break relations with South Africa and the dam of vituperation burst.

In retrospect my time in Cairo coincided with the mid-
point of the decade which saw the high-water mark for the
Soviet Union and its allies in the most important of Arab
states, and the low-water mark for the West. Nasser had
broken through the web of Western domination with the
purchase of Russian arms, via Czechoslovakia, in 1955, following unsuccessful attempts to persuade the United States
to increase military supplies to Egypt. The following year
he had turned to the Soviet Union to construct the Aswan
High Dam after America and Britain had withdrawn their
pledge to the World Bank project. Suez had eliminated Britain and France from the Egyptian scene and Nasserite inspiration had helped to bring about the downfall of the
pro-Western monarchy in Iraq in 1958. In spite of American sympathy for the 1952 revolution and the part played
by President Eisenhower first in forcing Britain and France
to call off the Suez operation and secondly in obliging the
Israelis to withdraw from Sinai in 1957, the United States
was firmly in the doghouse by 1960. Although America was
supplying large quantities of cheap grain to Egypt, she received no thanks. The demands of positive neutrality and
non-alignment required an anti-American posture, exacer-
bated by growing American support for Israel and for the
regimes in the Arab world which were resisting the Nasserite onrush.

By contrast the Russians were riding high. In the world
of Embassies the Soviet Union and the Eastern Europeans
predominated. Russian military and technical advisers were
beginning to flood the country and the sparsely furnished
Cairo shopfronts exhibited a dingy collection of second-rate
Eastern European goods. Communist grandees came and
went on official visits: even Raoul Castro appeared for a
round of interminable Cuban-style anti-Yankee oratory.

The people of Cairo did not give the impression of
over-enthusiasm about their new friends. The Russians

kept very much to themselves and were wisely inconspicuous. They spent little money in the shops and had acquired a reputation for dour exclusiveness which did not endear them to the jovial Egyptians. Jokes abounded about the regime's subservience to Moscow. A man met a friend in the street with his umbrella up on a fine day. 'Why are you protecting yourself against rain which is not falling?' Answer: 'Didn't you hear this morning's weather report? It is raining in Moscow.'

Evidence of seventy years of British domination, ended only eight years previously, was hard to find. The heart of Cairo had always owed more to Ottoman-French architecture and French town planning than to British influence. The whole ambience was Mediterranean and cosmopolitan rather than that of the North Sea. French was more prevalent as a second language than English, except for incipient Americanisation amongst the younger generation: years of British control over the educational system seemed to have left little mark. The bureaucratic and legislative systems were continental and systematised (at least in theory) rather than insular and pragmatic. Egyptian policemen resembled their Turkish counterparts rather than the products of Hendon and the London beat.

Not even in the Armed Forces, that most traditional element in most societies, could I detect the influence of Sandhurst and the succession of British Sirdars from Lord Kitchener onwards. The young Egyptian Commando and Parachute troops which could be seen exercising vigorously in the area of the Pyramids were a cross between the U.S. Marine Corps and the Red Army.

In 1960, I decided with some trepidation to join the pullulating mass of spectators at the military parade to celebrate Revolution Day. I hoped that I might be taken for an Eastern European visitor, but I took the additional precaution of carrying my daughter on my shoulders as insurance against any unfriendly manifestations. Immediately I heard the word 'Inglesi' being bandied about amongst the throng of working- and middle-class Egyptians which surrounded me. My daughter was seized from my shoulders and passed forward to the front of the crowd so that she could get a better view of the parade, and I was subjected to a volley of friendly badinage about the quality of the Russian equipment which, my interlocutors assured me, was vastly superior to the obsolete rubbish which the British had fobbed off on the Egyptian army. There was no hostility, even when I revealed myself as a British diplomat, towards the representative of a nation with which Egypt had so recently been at war.

The parade itself bore no resemblance to the Trooping of the Colour. Line after line of tanks, artillery, armoured cars, lorries and infantry ground heavily past, each unit greeted with loud cheers in which I sometimes thought I detected a note of good-humoured mockery. Squadrons of Russian aircraft flew past. Towards the end, the skies cleared of aircraft. Suddenly a small, rather stout, jet aircraft roared over the crowd to ringing applause. I asked my new acquaintances what was so remarkable about this apparition. I was told that it was the new Egyptian-built fighter, the Nasser (I think it was called), a symbol of Egypt's new-found independence of the great powers. I learnt later that it had been assembled near Cairo to a Spanish design. I never saw another and doubt whether the Nasser ever saw service in the Air Force.

Apart from the purely British institutions such as the Anglican Cathedral, still standing proudly on the East bank of the Nile but with its congregation reduced to a handful, the strongest evidence of Britain's brief moment of power in the long history of Egypt was to be found in the clubs, in particular the famous Gezira Club on Zamalek Island. Next door to the racecourse, originally an adjunct of the Club, the Gezira still breathed a powerful atmosphere of the British Indian Raj. Tennis courts, swimming pools, a golf course, an adequate clubhouse and, believe it or not, a cricket field: all this had survived revolution, war and now positive neutrality and non-alignment. Mercifully the decaying snobbery and British exclusiveness of the Alwiyah and Railway Clubs of Baghdad had disappeared. The membership was mixed: Egyptian military officers, foreign diplomats, Egyptian and foreign journalists, academics and professional men, all with their wives and families, mingled

happily and without inhibition. Only the Eastern Europeans
stood aloof, solemnly playing volleyball in a corner of the
old football field where I had watched British officers playing rugby football in far-off, wartime days. The children
played in the playgrounds, their sandwiches still being
snatched from their hands by the rapacious grey crows
which had always haunted the place. Tea and drinks were
dispensed on the terraces where bridge players sat absorbed
from morning to evening. My wife and I played tennis there
almost daily, mainly with our friends in the Egyptian and
foreign press corps. We even had an annual treat – an international tennis tournament in which the British perform-
ers played their modest and not very successful part.
Pietrangeli, the Italian star, was the hero of the crowd and
the best Egyptian players accepted defeat gracefully at his
hands. And we actually revived cricket. The indomitable
Geoffrey Arthur, a great enthusiast for the game, discovered
the two or three Egyptian professionals who had devotedly
maintained the ground and equipment through the blank
years. There they were, old Mahmoud, still a high-class
off-spin bowler and young Shaban, a valuable all-rounder;
both of Minor Counties standard. The nets were set up and
practice began. We had no difficulty in raising teams. There
were plenty of us in the Mission who were keen to play,
plus some admirable Indians, Pakistanis and Australians; in
the holidays our talents were supplemented by English
boys, including my own, out for the holidays from their
boarding-schools.

We also had a good Egyptian turnout, mainly alumni of
Victoria College in Alexandria, a public school (by that time
nationalised) originally created by the British business community, and the alma mater of many distinguished Egyptians
and Arabs including King Hussein of Jordan. Was Victoria
perhaps one of our principal legacies? Anyway it produced
some good cricketers who were keen on a game. One elderly
Coptic gentleman, who had taken an Egyptian touring side
to England in the 1920s, turned out regularly and (am I
imagining it?) I think the great Omar Sharif played a few
times. Being ahead of our time we normally played
limited-over games – on matting wickets on grass – and the

standard was by no means contemptible. It was the greatest
fun.

In spite of our political and administrative difficulties –
the God Hercules himself would have found the labour of
dealing with the Egyptian bureaucratic machine almost beyond his powers – time passed very agreeably for us. Apart
from our many Egyptian and foreign friends and the cosy
intimacy of the Mission, there was a great deal more to do
than taking vigorous exercises at the Gezira Club. Cairo
was overcrowded and the glitter of the old days had gone.
But it was still colourful and full of life – the people were
apparently impervious to the grey solemnities of Eastern
socialism. The bazaars, mosques and gardens were places
of enchantment and the Bolshoi Ballet a worthy successor
to *Aida* in the old Opera House, since burnt down. My wife
and sons – I am personally terrified of horses – used to ride
regularly in the desert between the Pyramids of Giza and
Saqqara and we had the bonus of being able to use our old
Consulate at Suez – no deal having been struck on a mutual
exchange of consular relations – as a weekend cottage for
swimming expeditions in the Red Sea. The beaches of
Alexandria were within easy reach and ex-King Farouk's
palace there was open to the public, a nauseating display of
opulent bad taste down to his dress shirts and tailcoats.

As we toured the country, I began to realise what had
happened to Alexandria. A strongly centralised, totalitarian
government exercises a magnetism which draws all forms
of activity to the capital. Where nothing can be done without the involvement of the state, those who are not close to
the centre of power move into limbo and decline. Cairo was
where the action was taking place and it was to Cairo that
rich and poor gravitated, whether bankers, industrialists,
officials, academics, professional men, or villagers from the
already overcrowded Delta and Nile Valley. Occasionally
the government would launch a so-called decentralisation
campaign but this was as futile as the political constructs
which the people had learned to disregard. If you were to
succeed you had to be close to the military gentlemen who
ran the country, or close to someone who had direct or
indirect access to them.

69

The months passed and the rhetorical storms flashed and thundered above the heads of the patient Egyptians. The Union was clearly in trouble. It had been forced on a reluctant Nasser in 1958 by panic-stricken Syrian nationalists fearing a Communist take-over, and the glow of propaganda about its success grew more lurid as the evidence mounted of unrest in Damascus and indifference in Cairo. British policy in Aden and the Gulf was routinely castigated but the Americans, for no particularly good reason, became the principal victims of vituperative blasts. President Kennedy fared worse than President Eisenhower. His speeches were ignored by the Cairo press, now nationalised, and the Press Attaché at the American Embassy spent an uncomfortable night at a police station for daring to distribute copies in Arabic of a particularly important statement by the President which had been ignored by the local media. Our American colleagues used regularly to compare notes with us about which of our two countries was currently heading Nasser's league of public hatred. However, the American Embassy was not prepared nonchalantly to accept this situation and to laugh it off as we did, any annoyance we might feel being tempered by the knowledge, as was the case with the Americans, that the actualities of Cairo's policy towards both of us differed radically from the impression created by these torrid blasts of obloquy. We would never have contemplated driving round Cairo dumping piles of texts of speeches on park benches, etc., the exercise which led to the detention of the American Press Attaché. We would not have dreamed of wasting time and money on producing a daily newspaper in Arabic, as did the United States Information Services. Perhaps we were wrong to be so dismissive, although, lacking the financial resources to mount an information effort on anything like the scale of the Americans, we had no choice. But I still think that the United States underestimated the scepticism of their Egyptian audiences who tended to dismiss anything which emanated from any governmental source as being as mendacious as the effusions of their own authorities. Or they would just laugh.

In 1961 the American Embassy was instructed to publicise President Kennedy's newly created Peace Corps. A film was sent to the U.S.S.R. for showing to as wide an audience as could be mustered. My wife and I attended the first night in company with a large number of Egyptians. I cannot remember much of the film but one passage is imprinted on my memory. A scene was shown of American Peace Corps teachers instructing a roomful of West African children in the mysteries of literacy in the English language. The lesson ended with a song, of which the chorus ran as follows: 'The board is black, the chalk is white. Together we learn to read and write, read and write.' The gale of laughter which swept over the Egyptians in the audience must have made their American hosts wonder whether they would not have done better to find a more sophisticated presentation of the Peace Corps and its activities for distribution to Cairo.

Meanwhile we advanced slowly and painfully towards our goal of a restoration of full diplomatic relations. Gradually the obstacles were removed and, in early 1961, an exchange of Ambassadors was agreed. We became the British Embassy again; Colin Crowe departed, his task successfully completed, and those of us who were left trooped to the airport to welcome our new Ambassador, Sir Harold Beeley. Nearly ten years previously he and I had served together in Baghdad where he had been Counsellor of the Embassy. Harold Beeley was another inspired choice. Intellectually brilliant, he had come to diplomacy from the academic world of Oxford and had gained considerable experience of the Middle East and its problems, particularly during the last three years of the Palestine Mandate when he had worked closely with Ernest Bevin. An extremely likeable and gregarious man, it was a certainty, as with Colin Crowe in his different way, that he would get on excellently with the Egyptians. So it proved: in fact he did two separate tours as Ambassador, an almost unique experience, and eventually retired from Cairo in 1971 with a towering reputation as one of the architects of the new, more relaxed and normal relationship between London and Cairo.

As spring turned to summer, the thoughts of the regime turned inward. The domestic political experiment had

bogged down: the National Union was roaring on the runway but showing no signs of taking to the air. The Syrian
region was turbulent – I started to think of my bet in Jordan
that it would last two years and no more – and Nasser
despatched Field-Marshal Abdul Hakim Amer, his closest
confidant, to Damascus to bring the situation under control.
The principal organ of 'national guidance', the weekly column 'Frankly Speaking' written in the newspaper *Al
Ahram* by Mohammed Hassanein Heikal, the journalist
closest to Nasser's thinking, began to prepare the public for
a major initiative. It came in June, a massive programme of
nationalisation which left little of the economy in private
hands. Would it work? We analysed it carefully and reported in cautiously favourable terms. But we wondered
whether the infrastructure of manpower, and the ramshackle state of the bureaucracy, would be sufficient to
cope with this additional burden.

By this time my own departure from Cairo was pending.
I had been continuously abroad for nearly seven years and
had spent the greater part of the previous sixteen years
either in the Middle East or working on Middle Eastern
affairs in England. I was nearly forty years old and felt that
the time had come for a change, preferably a few years in
London working on some area of the world totally uncon-
nected with my own specialisation.

My wife returned to England in the spring of 1961 leaving me to follow in the late summer, a longer separation
than we had experienced throughout our thirteen years of
marriage. I was seriously thinking of leaving diplomacy for
the academic world, and we also had a romantic notion of
running a village post office on the side. My wife was
briefed to reconnoitre these prospects while I continued the
argument with the Foreign Office about my next posting,
which had precipitated our decision to quit government
service. Fortunately I had a great deal of work to do, what
with a new Ambassador, the expansion of the operational
content of our dealings with the government, and the serious developments which were taking place within the
U.A.R. My friends, Egyptians, American and European,
saw to it that I was fully occupied in my leisure hours on

the tennis court and in political discussion around the lunch and dinner tables. Time passed quickly.

Shortly before my departure, an intriguing development took place which, in retrospect, symbolised the calmer future of Anglo-Egyptian relations. The Iraqi regime of General Abdul Karim Qasim, the 'unique leader', was threatening the integrity of the state of Kuwait which had only recently emerged from British protection. Successive Iraqi governments, even under the monarchy, had laid claim to Kuwait, and Qasim was blocking Kuwait's application to join the Arab League. There were Iraqi troop movements between Basra and the Kuwaiti frontier. The Amir invited Britain to send troops to protect his state and we responded positively.

On the face of it, this initiative should have aroused a tempest of hostility in the U.A.R. British forces had landed on Arab soil to protect a traditional, monarchist regime against a republican, revolutionary, socialist Arab government. Surely this would be the casus belli which would undo all our painstaking efforts of the previous three years.

Far from it. Although Nasser was blasting away incessantly at the traditional regimes of the Arabian peninsula, Qasim too had been admitted to the catalogue of U.A.R. demonology. Within a year or two of the Iraqi revolution of 1958, the Nasserite supporters amongst Qasim's military colleagues had been eliminated and the old rivalry between Baghdad and Cairo had been revived. The last thing the U.A.R. government wanted to see was the militant 'unique leader' gaining control of one of the richest oil states of the Gulf. At last British and Egyptian interests had come together and our military action took place without criticism, public or private, and with relatively little comment. The dawn of a new era was at hand.

In August 1961, I flew back to London after a long, debilitating but enjoyable round of farewells. I looked forward eagerly to being reunited with my family but I left Egypt with great sadness. I had come to love the country and the people: I had made many friends: our diplomacy had just entered a happier phase, and I had become personally involved in the fortunes of the regime. For all its failings and absurdities, for all the mistakes, the grotesque propaganda, the bombast and the attempts to dragoon an individualistic and cynical populace into a semblance of socialist order, I was sensitive of the underlying seriousness and good intentions of Nasser and the best of his colleagues, military and technocratic. I had been privileged to serve in what is, and has been for thousands of years, a great country.

In the event the disagreement between myself and the Foreign Office about my future was resolved and I stayed on. I was allowed an interlude from my Middle Eastern life, being appointed to the American Department of the Foreign Office. After reading the *Encyclopaedia Britannica* articles on each of the twenty-odd states in Latin America, a region of which I was sadly ignorant, I arrived at my desk in the early autumn with feelings of some trepidation.

Twenty-four years later

I can see now, looking back down the passage of twenty-four years, how fortunate I was to have served in Egypt at the time I did. Egypt, that most ancient of nation states and empires, has had a history of stability and conservative resistance to change unrivalled in the rest of the world, not only in Africa and Western Asia. Since the great Muslim Empire fragmented in the tenth century AD, Egypt has had only four different regimes, namely the Fatimid Caliphs, Mamelukes of various kinds, the dynasty founded by Mohammed Ali Pasha in 1805 and the Presidential system originated by the revolution of 1952 which, two years later, brought President Nasser to power. I experienced life in Egypt at first hand briefly as a soldier in the last years of the monarchy and then, as a diplomat, in what turned out to be the apogee of Nasserism. Thus I was present during one of the rare moments of change in that country in the previous thousand years. By the same token I was able to observe the denouement of the very brief, by Egyptian standards, period of British domination (a mere seventy years) and the birth of genuine independence in the contemporary sense of the word, under the first native

Egyptian rulers since the days of the Pharaohs. I could hardly have chosen a better time or, rather, chance could hardly have chosen a better time for me.

Now I ask myself: how much real change has there been? For fifteen years or so Nasser projected Egypt on to a larger stage with his so-called 'Philosophy of the Revolution': he was a co-author, with Nehru, Soekarno and Tito, of the concept of 'positive neutrality and non-alignment'. He carried Egypt into the mainstream of Arab and African politics and helped to restore to the Arab peoples, from Morocco to the frontiers of Iran, the dignity and self-respect which they had lost during centuries of submission to Turkish rule followed by decades of subservience to European patronage. His obsession with freeing Egypt from the spectre of British imperialism certainly accelerated the disappearance of that phenomenon, leaving scarcely a trace on the Egyptian canvas on which generations of British officers and officials had worked so hard.

Nevertheless, although Nasser briefly shook the world outside Egypt's borders, he found himself confronted by more resistant material in his own people. Politically his experiments in 'grass roots' democracy failed and he was obliged, willy nilly, to adopt the Pharaonic, one-man, heroic style of government with which the people of Egypt as a whole seem to feel most comfortable. Economically his excursion into socialist state ownership of production and services was ill-received in concept and ineffective in practice. His programme of land reforms broke the power of certain great families but it was circumvented to a great extent by multiple ownership of a series of small plots amongst members of the same extended families: it certainly failed to transform the peasant nature of most of Egypt's agriculture. His (and the Soviet Union's) monument to history, the Aswan High Dam, has probably proved to be an asset rather than a liability, although even this is open to question. And, by the end of his life, his foreign policies, the foundation of his great prestige, were disintegrating. His quest for Arab unity had burnt itself out: his insistence on leadership of the Arabs against Israel had led him into a tragic error in 1967 which not only left the Arab armies shattered and

Israel in occupation of further large stretches of Arab territory, but also changed the balance between the socialist and the traditional oil-rich Arab states, leaving the former suing for the favours of the latter in order to rebuild their economies and their military machines. He died in 1970, exhausted and probably disillusioned, while in the process, not of leading the Arab world in a fresh diplomatic or military initiative, but of acting as a peacemaker between the one-time target of his abuse and contempt, King Hussein, and the leader of the newly reborn Palestinian national movement, Yasser Arafat.

In most countries where there is no constitutional provision for peaceful change of government, the unexpected death of a leader of Nasser's calibre would have unleashed a bloody power struggle, probably military intervention. But this did not happen in Egypt. His long-standing, but not widely respected, colleague, Anwar Sadat, succeeded him and, after some skilful manoeuvring behind the scenes, achieved an absolutist, personal supremacy analogous to that of Nasser. For a time the memory of the dead hero was venerated, but evidence of what came inelegantly to be known as 'denasserification' began shortly to accumulate. Sadat restored Arab military honour in the Arab/Israeli war of October 1973 and opened the way to eventual peace negotiations between Egypt and Israel. As had happened in the 1840s when Mohammed Ali Pasha had been obliged to withdraw from Syria and the Lebanon, Egypt began to withdraw from its pan-Arab role into a more traditional, nilotic isolation. Sadat regained the Egyptian territory of Sinai at the expense of the unity of the Arab League under Egyptian leadership, and committed his country to economic recovery with the support of the West in general and the United States in particular. Nasser's socialist economic measures were dismantled and Egypt reverted to a style of entrepreneurial capitalism reminiscent to many Egyptians of the days of King Farouk. The personal austerity practised by Nasser and certain of his leading associates gave way to an imperial and plutocratic ostentation comparable to that associated in the public mind with the Cairo of previous generations.

1 River view of Baghdad, 1953

2 Sheila Parsons being presented to King Hussein of Jordan at
the coronation of King Faisal II in Baghdad, 1953

3 *Left*, Anthony Parsons's daughter, Emma, and elder son in Amman, 1959

4 *Below*, his wife and sons riding near the Pyramids, Cairo, 1961

Egypt

Sadat became increasingly the antithesis of Nasser. Where the latter had identified with the Soviet Union and with the anti-Western face of the non-aligned movement, Sadat became the darling of the United States who adopted him and his attractive wife as honorary Americans, quintessential 'goodies' who had dared to make peace with America's regional protégé, Israel, and to turn their backs on socialism and the adversaries of the 'free world'. American civil and military aid poured into Egypt (although the cornucopia was never opened to the extent that it was for Israel).

But the economic situation failed to improve to an extent consonant with Sadat's promises. How could it, even with newly found Egyptian self-sufficiency in oil? The population explosion blew away the benefits of aid and of the renascent private sector. Furthermore, Sadat and his American allies failed to deliver progress towards a solution to the Palestine problem and he was publicly denounced as a traitor for selling the Arab cause for the sake of the recovery of Sinai. The American connexion and the reversion of the nouveau riche to ostentation and corruption added fuel to the flames burning in the breasts of the more devout and passionate urban Egyptians. In 1981 Sadat was assassinated by disaffected soldiers in a military parade: appropriately his life ended as so much of it had been conducted in the previous two or three years, under the cameras of Western television.

Even this bloody event failed to disturb Egypt's monumental serenity. Vice-President Hosni Mubarak succeeded Anwar Sadat without fuss or resistance. The Egyptian caravan moved on as it moves on today, overloaded with surplus population, burdened with economic problems, still partially alienated from the other Arab caravans, but drawing steadily closer to some of them, less noisy and boisterous than it was under Nasser or Sadat, less totally committed in its external relations, less colourful but for all that perhaps more reliable and less prone to accident.

Yes, there have been changes in Egypt. The cosmopolitan minorities who dominated Egyptian politics for part of the British period have disappeared and Egypt is at last ruled by its own people. The nationalist spirit which struggled for supremacy from the last days of the nineteenth century has found fulfilment, thanks to Nasser and his strong drive for true independence. But much remains from the more distant past. The people of Egypt, easy-going, long-suffering and with their roots reaching deep into the social and economic imperatives of the Nile Valley, have refused to be transmuted into dynamic revolutionaries and, more than thirty years later, the dramatic event of 1952 can be seen more as a change from a regime which had run its course than a fundamental upheaval like the revolution of 1979 in Iran. In its foreign policy Egypt has, at least for the time being, reverted to its association with the Western world which began with Napoleon's invasion in 1798. For a short time the Soviet Embassy assumed the primacy held for many years by the British Embassy. Since the early 1970s that not entirely enviable position has been shouldered by the United States of America. Britain has more friendly relations with Egypt today than at any time during the past century, but is of less consequence than France. As long ago as the 1930s an American academic at the American University in Cairo, Mr Russell Galt, included the following sentence in a pamphlet he wrote: 'In Egypt England had an army – the French an idea. England had educational control – France a clear educational philosophy. Because the French did have such an organised philosophy and the English did not, the French pen has proved mightier than the English sword.'

FOUR

The Sudan

I cannot say that I was overjoyed when I was told, in the early autumn of 1963, that I had been appointed Head of Chancery in the Embassy in Khartoum. We had spent two happy years in London and I was looking forward to a third, hoping that, when I next went abroad, it would be on promotion. My two sons were in the process of changing schools and my daughter was doing well in the Junior Department of the James Allens School in Dulwich. I had become absorbed in the intricacies of British relations with Latin America: there were plenty of interesting problems to work on. The Cuban missile crisis of 1962 had added a dramatic dimension to my desk, and I had gained experience of a number of subjects which were to recur in my life in the future – trade promotion, the Falklands, British Honduras (Belize), political systems in Latin America and the essentials of Anglo-American relations, being only some. However, on this occasion, I lost the argument about my career and we set off for Khartoum in the first days of 1964. This journey should have been the first in our married life when we would experience the luxury of travelling by ourselves, that is to say without any small children. Our sons were at their public school and, because of the lack of adequate education for foreigners in the Sudan, we had reluctantly despatched our daughter, now eight years old, to the junior school of Bedales, the coeducational school in Hampshire.

But we were not destined to enjoy a relaxed and comfortable flight to Khartoum. We had with us in a basket my daughter's beloved Siamese cat, nicknamed the Ass because of his low intelligence and idiotic hyper-activity. Although we had booked him to travel in the cabin with us (and had

had the booking confirmed), we ran into a road-block at the check-in counter at Heathrow. An official told me that the cat would have to travel in the hold. It seemed that some other passenger wanted to take a dog. Only one animal was supposed to be in the cabin and dogs, in this Englishman's view, took precedence over cats. I lost my temper and an exchange of buffets between myself and the airline official was only narrowly avoided by the intervention of some apprehensive fellow travellers. After further discussion the case was decided in the cat's favour and we set off.

Apart from the cat in his basket and our hand luggage, we were also, for obvious reasons, carrying a tray of cat litter, a grey and granulated concoction. When the aircraft landed in transit in Tripoli, Libya, my wife and I made a determined but unsuccessful attempt to persuade the Ass to relieve nature. Admitting defeat, we wandered into the transit lounge to have some coffee, leaving the litter tray outside. When the time came to re-embark, the tray had disappeared. At the time we did not regard this as a serious deprivation. We just wondered why anybody should have bothered to steal it, and what treasure the thief imagined it to contain. It was only when we arrived in Khartoum in the early hours of the following morning that we appreciated the magnitude of our loss.

As we emerged from the aircraft, I smelt an unfamiliar smell – earthy, pungent and humid: the scent of Africa. Admittedly Egypt, our last post, is on the African continent but this was new, different and intriguing. In spite of the lateness of the hour, Robert Walmsley, Counsellor of the Embassy, and his wife, plus Rab and Annette Munro, the Commercial Counsellor and his wife, old friends from Baghdad days, were there to meet us. The Walmsleys – later to become very dear friends of ours – we had not met before. They had arranged for us to spend the night – or what was left of it – with them. A very kind gesture, we thought, as we were shown into a spotlessly clean and comfortable spare room, and what a relief to be able to get into bed after our long journey without having to suffer the embarrassment, caused so often in the past, by our usual baggage train of small, tired, over-excited children. Then it was that we remembered the loss of the Ass's lavatory.

His natural functions had been paralysed by the journey, but it was only reasonable to assume that he was, by this time, bursting. I crept down to the garden with him where his reaction to Africa was even more pronounced than mine had been at the airport. With a wild Siamese cry he flung himself at me and we returned indoors, by this time on the worst terms. We were terrified of his befouling the beautiful spare room, so we locked him in the adjoining bathroom. This he didn't like at all and showed his displeasure by emitting very loud, high-pitched, human-like shrieks. We were then terrified of his waking up our hosts, so we brought him back into the bedroom. A sleepless night followed for both of us. Whenever we heard the Ass stirring, the only solution seemed to be to rush him into the bathroom and go through the absurdity of holding the brute over the lavatory like a baby, all to no avail. It was a relief when the sun rose and we could get up: to be fair to the cat he had managed to hold himself in check for the best part of twenty-four hours. Who was it who said that diplomatic life was nothing but a luxurious bed of roses?

Head of Chancery is a post peculiar to the British Diplomatic Service. He or she runs the political and general section of the Embassy and is responsible for staff management and overall supervision of the administration; as well as acting as a kind of chief of staff or factotum to the Ambassador and, depending on the personalities, to the Ambassador's wife. With a pompous and demanding Ambassador and an unhappy staff the interest of the political work is vitiated by the hellish nature of the other duties. There were no such problems in Khartoum. The Ambassador and his wife, Ian and Drusilla Scott, were charming and unpretentious while the largish staff, as is so often the case in remote and isolated posts, seemed to have few problems of morale. I settled in quickly.

For nearly a century the Sudan had occupied a romantic corner in the imagination of the British. Annexed by the Egyptian government in the 1820s, mainly as a source of slaves from the non-Muslim south, the Sudanese had always been restive under alien domination. In the 1880s a religious leader had arisen, the Mahdi, and had captured Khartoum in 1885 after a siege in which the defender (for the Egyptian government), General Gordon, had acquired legendary fame. The Mahdi himself died shortly after the fall of Khartoum. Thereafter, for thirteen years, his successor, the Khalifa, had ruled the Sudan as the first truly independent Arab state in modern times. Friendless and continually menaced by Anglo-Egyptian pressure, the Khalifa had held out – and had at one stage taken the initiative in invading Egypt – until his army, fighting with dauntless courage, had been destroyed by the automatic fire of Lord Kitchener's forces at the battle of Omdurman in 1898. Thereafter the Sudan had been ruled as an Anglo-Egyptian condominium for nearly sixty years, finally regaining its independence in 1956.

The democratic, presidential constitution bequeathed by the British had quickly foundered on the rocks of faction between the principal political groups – one pro-Egyptian and the other comprising the sectarian adherents to the Mahdist family and tradition, the Ansar – which were deeply divided in mutual antipathy. In 1958 the Army lost patience and a military coup brought a junta to power headed by General Abboud, still President when I arrived in Khartoum. After a brief interlude of civilian government, the Sudanese had exchanged their experience of British direct rule for rule by their own military with only vestigial traces, the technical Ministers, of civilian involvement. There appeared to be no plans for an early return of democracy.

It did not take me long to form a number of impressions. First, in contrast to Egypt, there was no mistaking the imprint of Britain. Khartoum itself had been laid out on geometrical lines radiating from the Governor-General's (now the President's) Palace, on the pattern of imperial cantonments the eastern world over. To the north of the Blue Nile lay Khartoum North, the home of light industry and new housing estates, and to the west of the White Nile – the city lies at the confluence of the two rivers – was the swarming labyrinth of Omdurman: in all a classic pattern recognisable to anyone familiar with, say, Peshawur.

The only European second language was English – most subjects in Khartoum University were still taught in the English language – and the educated classes spoke, read and wrote it with an ease and fluency comparable only to the standard in a Commonwealth country. The civilian bureaucracy was less cumbersome and systematised than in the other Arab states, more akin to our own simpler procedures. The Army and Police, in appearance, style and manner, not to speak of armament, emitted powerful echoes of their British-trained past: the Sudanese retained British officers in certain advisory posts, and the civil airline was almost entirely operated by British subjects. More than anywhere else where I had served I saw that Britain had bequeathed a varied legacy, and not a bad one, to this country.

The evening after our arrival, we had our first taste of British cultural influence. The Ambassador and his wife took us to see a performance of *School for Scandal* by the Omdurman High School for Girls. It was a hot night – the Sudan is an equatorial country and there is no month in the year when the shade temperature does not exceed 100° – and the play was staged out of doors. It was an outlandish and moving scene. In the still, African night, pierced with the shrill of cicadas and the croaking of a million frogs, the adolescent Sudanese girls, in powdered wigs and elaborate English eighteenth-century costumes, vigorously acted out this elegant comedy of manners. Their English pronunciation may not have been that of the age of reason in London and their round, black faces poured with sweat as the action intensified; but there was no mistaking their enjoyment of their performance. It was memorable.

It may be that the certainties of direct rule leave less of a bitter aftertaste than the shadowy suspicions excited by indirect rule, as in Egypt or Iraq. It may be that there is something special about the character of the Sudanese, that mixture of Arab and African blood. Whatever the reason, the Sudanese did not seem to have the same chip on the shoulder with which I had become familiar elsewhere in the region. General Gordon's statue had been removed to

Chatham from its place of honour in front of the Presidential Palace but the older generation still referred to the University of Khartoum as Gordon College and, perhaps with conscious irony, the only night-club in Khartoum was named the Gordon.

Our Sudanese friends and colleagues treated us with bluff and genial equality and I became accustomed to the look of faintly amused affection in their eyes. I recall being asked by the Ambassador to interest the Ministry of Education in the newly created Voluntary Service Overseas. I called on one of the Under-Secretaries and waded laboriously through an account of the virtues of those young men and women who were prepared to teach English in Sudanese schools for little more than pocket money (shades of 'the board is black, the chalk is white'). The Under-Secretary listened patiently but I could detect a sardonic expression forming on his face. When I had finished, he thought for a moment and replied, 'Yes, I understand what you are offering – underdeveloped Englishmen for underdeveloped countries.' A bellow of laughter followed this sally, robbing it of any possible offence.

The most remarkable manifestation of Sudanese tolerance of their former imperial masters was the continued existence of the Sudan Club, another Raj-style legacy of the Empire. The Club occupied several acres of land in the centre of Khartoum. It had a swimming pool and a large number of grass tennis courts, extensive gardens and an imposing clubhouse, in a state of progressive dilapidation. The membership was entirely British plus, I think, old Commonwealth with maybe some foreign diplomats as honorary members. No Sudanese was allowed to enter the premises apart from the Club servants, groundsmen, etc. Given the small size of Khartoum, the situation was analogous to the Americans having annexed and fenced off the whole of Hyde Park, called it the Britain Club and denied entry to all except American citizens.

And yet successive Sudanese independent governments had made no move either to close it down and to annex the Club and its premises, or to insist that it be thrown open to Sudanese. Perhaps, in their wisdom, they judged it better to allow the large British community to disport itself according to British customs on this luxurious reservation, rather than having them swamp the limited amenities of the city. Needless to say, intermittent guerrilla warfare raged between the Embassy and the Club Committee. The Ambassador was determined to persuade the Club to relax its restrictions on membership; the Committee was equally determined to die in the last ditch in defence of the Club's exclusiveness. There was no meeting of minds and, by the time I left, the Committee's rearguard action was still holding out.

Wherever I went I found deep affection for individual members of the old Sudan Political Service who had ruled the country for so long; no resentment either that we had bloodily extinguished Sudanese independence at Omdurman, in the lifetime of the fathers and grandfathers of many of those with whom we were in contact. Lord Kitchener was cordially detested, not for the casualties which his Maxims had inflicted, but for his subsequent desecration of the Mahdi's tomb. Gordon was held in some respect as a brave and high-principled man. The most touching monument to this historical episode was the Khalifa's house in Omdurman, a simple mud-brick structure, now a museum. In it were displayed the memorabilia of the period, including the pitifully inadequate firearms with which the Sudanese had confronted the Anglo-Egyptian regular forces. Most heartbreaking of all were the terrible lists of casualties, tens of thousands of dead and wounded from the battlefield which lay in the open countryside outside the city much as it had been after the engagement over sixty years previously.

My second impression was of how little we had done for the Sudan by way of economic development in more than half a century of our rule. There was admittedly a large cotton plantation which had been developed at Wad Medani, south-east of Khartoum, but this was designed to supply raw cotton to British mills, not to feed an indigenous textile industry. There were some minor irrigation works, and single-track railways ran north to Egypt and east to Port Sudan. But the capital was an island in a vast desert: there were only a few miles of paved roads. The agricultural potential of the land was obvious from the tall grass which grew almost overnight after heavy tropical rain, but no capital investment had been poured in to exploit this. The villages were still sunk in primeval poverty, and virtually all the scanty industrial and communications development had taken place in the few years following independence. We had ruled competently and sympathetically; we had administered adequately and had imposed law and order on a divided and turbulent land; we had protected the territorial integrity of the Sudan from external predators: but we had done little to raise the standard of living of the people. This brought home to me the novelty of the concept of 'foreign aid'. Until the 1950s British dependent territories had to exist on their local resources. If rich, that was their good luck; if poor, that was too bad. The Metropolitan power felt no obligation to mulct its own taxpayers to relieve the poverty of others. I believe that it was only in the late 1940s that the Colonial Office established a department named Colonial Development and Welfare and it was as late as 1961 that the Government created a special Department responsible for Overseas Aid. One of my jobs in Khartoum was to administer a small, but growing, aid programme to the Sudan under the aegis of this Department and its successor, the Ministry for Overseas Development.

My third impression, contrary to what I had learnt of the character of the Sudanese people, was of the apathetic, depressed atmosphere in Khartoum. There were of course many exceptions, but the bulk of the population went about their business listlessly and without the laughter and jollity which I had been told to anticipate. The regime, although basically benevolent and lacking in the harshness normally associated with military dictatorships, was disposed to run the country as if it were a battalion of infantry: this blanket on public expression had exercised a suffocating influence on national morale, suggesting serious discontent below the surface. There were no riots or demonstrations and political parties were banned: military discipline had seen to that. But the malaise was palpable and I could not help feeling that there was combustible material about. And the problem of the South preoccupied the politically conscious. The southern provinces of the Sudan are inhabited by African tribes who have nothing in common ethnically or in religious belief with the Muslim Arabs of the northern districts. A few had adopted Islam but the majority were either animist or Christian. During the condominium the British had lovingly administered the South but, in the view of the northerners, had failed to make any serious effort to integrate the two halves of the country. You ran the South as a human zoo, my Sudanese friends used to say with some bitterness.

The southerners had viewed with apprehension the prospect of being absorbed into an independent Arab state – Arabs had for centuries been the principal slave traders in East and Central Africa – and, by the early 1960s, a breakaway movement had emerged and the South was in a state of civil war. Engagements with the Army were frequent and casualties were mounting. To the hardline Muslims in Khartoum, concessions to southern autonomy were unthinkable, let alone secession. There was no solution in sight and the situation was complicated by the presence of about 50,000 southerners in Khartoum working mainly on construction sites, enormously tall men, scantily dressed and of daunting appearance. In early 1964, the government heightened the drama by summarily expelling all the Christian missionaries from the South (mainly Italians of the Verona Fathers Order) on the grounds that they were abetting subversion and terror. This move had no effect except to damage the international reputation of the Sudan.

Vast, poor and lacking in attractive natural resources such as oil, the Sudan was, however, important to Britain. Our main interest was in maintaining our overflying rights. Britain still had a chain of military installations and responsibilities in East Africa, in Aden, in the Persian Gulf and through to the Far East. Since the mid-1950s military aircraft had been unable to overfly Egypt or Syria. This left us with two lines of communication, one over our CENTO partners, Turkey and Iran, the other over Libya (with transit facilities at the R.A.F. base at El Adem) and the Sudan, avoiding Egyptian airspace. (Libya was of course governed by King Idris: Colonel Qaddafi had not been heard of.)

Without this southern route we would have been hard put to it. A few weeks after I arrived, the importance of this facility was put to the test. Army mutinies broke out in Kenya, Uganda and Tanzania immediately after independence and the three governments called on Britain to restore the situation. Had we not been able to fly troops in via the Sudan, it is difficult to see how we could have met this requirement. But we could and did, and all was well.

Overflying was by no means the only reason why Britain needed a friendly, stable and moderate government in Khartoum. The Sudan occupied an important geographical position bordering on the Arab world to the north, Ethiopia to the east and sub-Saharan Africa to the south and west. The Sudanese had an important voice in the recently formed Organisation for African Unity and British decolonisation in Africa was still incomplete: the problem of Southern Rhodesia was beginning to fester following the collapse of the Central African Federation. We needed a close dialogue with a friendly African government. Trade, investment and aid were other reasons, as was the presence of some thousands of British and British-protected subjects in the Sudan engaged in a multifarious variety of activities.

None of these topics presented severe problems to the Embassy in my first six months or so. My work took on a routine, unexciting tinge. Our leisure was agreeable enough, but limited. Tennis, swimming, boating and fishing on the two Niles, exploration of the countryside and getting to know our Sudanese colleagues occupied our time. Travel, with vast distances and poor roads, was arduous and the delights of the Gordon Night-Club and the two or three Khartoum hotels soon palled. It was, however, pleasant to live almost entirely in the open. The cinemas were open-air and we slept on the flat roof of our house. The weather was a diversion. The heat was never-ending but it was punctuated by torrential rain, thunderstorms which would have gratified King Lear's most extreme requirements, and a southerly wind, the Haboob, which brought with it a solid wall of black dust from the faraway cotton fields. I remember lying awake one night with one of the children on the roof when there was suddenly a smell of the Pit itself and what appeared to be a ball of fire exploded just above our heads; another occasion when we could see the Haboob approaching us like a wall of black: battening down the hatches was no use, minutes later the whole house was engulfed in black grit, which took days to clear away.

The Ass survived, albeit with difficulty. He soon became accustomed to roaming the garden at night. But the garden was full of mongooses and the idiot saw fit to open hostilities with one. He was bitten through the face, leaving him with a permanent sneer. And then he contracted cat flu and, after days of immobile moribundity, disappeared in the middle of a thunderstorm. I advertised for him in the Arabic newspapers with the offer of a modest reward for his recovery. Two days later a Sudanese lorry driver arrived at the door carrying what looked like a drowned rat. The invalid was back, at the point of death. We rushed him to our expert Sudanese vet and the Ass's heart stopped on the table. Undaunted, the vet injected a powerful substance into his heart and he revived. A few days later he was back to breaking our ornaments as if nothing had been wrong with him. He survived to die a few years later of pneumonia at a respectable age, in our next post, Bahrain.

Of our trips around the country, the visit I remember most vividly was made to the new settlement of Khashm el Girba in the eastern Sudan near the border with Ethiopia. The Aswan High Dam in Egypt had been completed and Lake Nasser was beginning to fill; it would eventually inundate the town of Wadi Halfa and the surrounding Sudanese villages. Tens of thousands of Sudanese had to be moved and the empty area of Khashm el Girba had been chosen as their new home. The government had done its best. Irrigation canals had been dug to water the arid wasteland, and breezeblock townships – looking like Welsh mining villages in a recession – were beginning to punctuate the illimitable skyline.

It was, to use Captain Scott's description of the South Pole, an awful place. A single-track railway passed through the area and parties of evacuees were being dumped at various points along the line. There they sat, resigned and passive, in the middle of higgledy-piggledy mounds of pathetic luggage and household belongings. Some were trailing off towards the grim, grey blockhouses of their new homes. Great caravans of nomads were passing and the irrigation canals were choked with the rotting corpses of their camels, sheep and goats, the casualties of what was apparently a long march.

The placidity of our uneventful life ended abruptly in the early autumn of 1964. The balloon went up and had not fully descended by the time I left Khartoum a year later. In this book I have avoided detailed description of political events in the countries in which I have served. My purpose, as I stated in the introductory chapter, has been to convey a general impression of the nature of the life and work of a junior and middle-rank British diplomat during the last days of what had been a period of British dominance; not to write a short, amateur history of the modern Middle East. But I hope that my readers will bear with me if I describe the course of the 1964 revolution in the Sudan in some detail.

It was a rare, almost unique event, the overthrow of a military government by the action of unarmed civilians. I have never seen an account of it published in English, or in Arabic for that matter, and it might be of interest to have on record what one eyewitness can recall of this drama, even though the passage of twenty years may have expunged some of the events from my mind and partially distorted the true picture. In parenthesis, I recalled the course of the revolution in the Sudan fourteen years later when I was Ambassador in Tehran and the people of Iran combined in a similar campaign of civil disobedience to bring down the apparently impregnable military-based regime of Shah Mohammed Reza Pahlavi. That is another story which I have already told in my last book.

The summer had passed peacefully enough in Khartoum. It was September and Khartoum University was beginning to reassemble for the autumn term. There was a disturbance on the campus and the police and students clashed. Shots were fired and one, possibly two, students were killed: certainly no more. The incident took place around midday and, by afternoon, small riots and demonstrations were swirling in the centre of the city. These consisted of little groups of students shouting and sporadically stoning passing cars. My wife and I ran the gauntlet in the early evening. It was not particularly frightening and the outbreaks were on a limited scale and seemingly uncoordinated. The general impression as night fell was that the police would be able to bring the city quickly under control and that life would return to normal.

The following day the situation had neither improved nor deteriorated and we began to wonder whether something more grave might be brewing. Rumours began to circulate that the old political parties, under the leadership of the Communist Party of the Sudan, had come together and formed a National Front to co-ordinate opposition to the military government. The Communist Party was the best organised and had for this reason taken the lead. At the other end of the spectrum was the Muslim Brotherhood, at that time a more intellectual and less fundamentalist body than its counterparts in Egypt, Jordan and Syria. In the centre were the two great movements which commanded the widest popular support, the Ansar (followers of the Mahdist tradition led by the grandson and great-grandson of the Mahdi himself) and the Khatmia, traditionally the party closest to and most favourably disposed towards Egypt. As in Iran fourteen years later, these various political forces made strange bedfellows and were united in one purpose only, to bring down the government of the day.

The rumoured National Front was constituted and immediately called for a nation-wide strike. At this point it is appropriate to observe that, had General Abboud and his colleagues been as ruthless as many of the military regimes in the Middle East and Africa, matters would not have been allowed to reach this point. At the first sign of trouble all the civilian political leaders would have been arrested and the Army would have moved decisively to pre-empt a spread of civil disturbance. Without leadership it is doubtful whether the campaign of passive resistance and withdrawal of co-operation could have been mounted. But the military leaders of the Sudan were not tyrants: they were decent, patriotic men who had felt obliged to intervene to rescue the country from the chaos into which the civilian politicians had plunged it. They did not have the stomach for a bloody confrontation with their own people and many of them would have welcomed a return to barracks and release from the frustrating exactions of their Cabinet posts. They were certainly in no mood to fight to the end in order to keep themselves in power.

Within twenty-four hours Khartoum had become a ghost city. The airport and civil airline closed and the railway company came out on strike. We were isolated. The state radio station shut down after announcing that it would come on the air again only to announce the resignation of the government. Shops, banks and offices closed. The committee organising the strike allowed one trainload of essential food supplies to come into Khartoum daily and services such as water, electricity and the telephone were maintained throughout. That was all.

The geography of the Sudan favoured the opposition. Khartoum was like an island in a sea of empty land dotted with small towns and villages. The South was preoccupied with its own problem, and the outlying centres of population in the northern areas could carry on for a time without the capital. But Khartoum was the seat of government and control of the state depended on control of Khartoum.

The military authorities were baffled. They tried to bring in reinforcements by train to overawe the populace; but the trains were on strike. They tried to bring in troops by air, but without military transport aircraft they were dependent on the civil airline, which was also on strike. In any case, what would the extra troops have done? The streets of the capital were empty and the government would not have contemplated house-to-house arrests and progressive execution of ringleaders until the strikers surrendered and returned to work.

For a few days the impasse persisted. It was a strange life. Social activity came to a standstill and day-to-day shopping for the necessities of life presented problems. My wife remembers ducking under the three-quarters-closed steel shutters of Greek-owned shops in order to buy our groceries: it was more a question of opening tins of sardines in the garden than attending brilliant diplomatic dinner parties. At night there was a curfew, originally imposed by the Army, and the city was wrapped in silence. Even the dogs kept the curfew. The chorus of barking which was a feature of normal night time died down; there was no movement of human beings to arouse the dogs and jackals. In the evenings, we used to sit for hours in our gardens or on our roofs, drinking whisky with visiting neighbours and speculating on what the next morning would bring. In many ways it was a pleasant time: we could see our close friends and talk to them without the distractions of large-scale entertainment and there was nothing to do except keep in touch with the British community and wait on events. At least there were no rioting mobs, no frenzied demonstrations, no risk to life and limb.

Less than a week later the tension broke. It was dark and we were as usual alert for the resumption of radio broadcasts. We missed the announcement itself but it suddenly became clear that the radio must have broadcast the resignation of the government. The silence of the night was broken by a great murmur of voices and the shuffling of thousands of feet. We rushed on to the roof to see what was happening. All across the city, as far as the eye could see, the streets and avenues were filling with white-robed, white-turbaned figures, each one carrying a burning torch or a palm branch or both. These streams of humanity were forming and flowing quietly towards the Presidential Palace with tributary rivulets diverting to the houses of opposition leaders. One of the leaders, the former Foreign Minister, Mohammed Ahmad Mahgoub, lived opposite our house across the narrow, unpaved street. Suddenly this street was thronged with dark-faced, white-clad Sudanese carrying their torches and palm branches. They had come to congratulate Mahgoub, peacefully and without excitement. The ex-Minister came out into the street and exchanged greetings with the crowd. We stood on the roof and watched, occasionally exchanging smiles and waves with the sea of faces and arms a few feet below us. It was a scene which I could not imagine taking place in any other capital city in which I had served, dramatic, dignified, archaic and intensely moving. Twenty years on, it is easy to recall to the mind's eye.

In the morning Khartoum was a place of rejoicing. There was no violence, only joy and relief. The sullenness of the past months and the tension of the past days had evaporated and a holiday atmosphere prevailed everywhere. The shops, the banks, the offices reopened and normal life resumed with the difference that there was a fresh feeling of good-humoured accomplishment and liberated energy in the air.

It would have been too much to expect in any country, that this denouement would have led to everyone living happily ever after. It soon emerged that the story was only beginning: before long, blood would flow. The politicians, united in their opposition to General Abboud and perhaps taken by surprise by the speed of their victory, had made no dispositions regarding a successor regime. Given the divergences in the political spectrum of the National Front, it was scarcely surprising that quarrels should break out about the distribution of power. They could not even form a caretaker cabinet and the country entered a period of limbo with the Army and the police maintaining basic order while the National Front continued to squabble: there was no government.

There followed an astonishing and tragic incident. The Embassy offices were in two upper floors of a building immediately opposite the gates of the Presidential Palace, separated from it by about a hundred yards of road and public gardens. One morning we saw that this open space was filling with the usual white-robed crowd carrying their palm branches. They were unarmed. After about a thousand, perhaps more, had gathered they began to chant slogans and to move towards the gate of the Palace. Troops with automatic weapons were deployed inside the gate and along the perimeter of the Palace garden. Reinforcements began to arrive from the garrison in South Khartoum. We saw a line of armoured cars moving slowly up the main avenue towards the Palace. Suddenly they stopped for a few minutes before resuming their advance and deploying along the Palace wall. Watching from our windows we were puzzled by the brief halt in the advance. We were later en-

lightened by a foreign journalist who had been accompanying the column. It seemed that, although the streets were
empty of all but the armoured column and the pedestrian
demonstrators, the officer in the leading armoured car had
halted his unit when the traffic lights in front of him had
turned to red! Another instance of a British legacy of civil
discipline.

Throughout the morning the chanting crowd swayed
backwards and forwards, up to the muzzles of the guns and
then retreating. The soldiers facing them looked uncomfortable but resolute. At about midday the doorbell of the
Embassy offices rang. I left my vantage point at the window
and answered it. A Sudanese was standing outside; he asked
politely to speak to the Ambassador. His message was that
the demonstration below had been organised by the Communist Party. They were sick of the squabblings of the
politicians and were determined to bring them to their
senses and to oblige them to form a government: hence the
demonstration outside the Palace. They had now decided to
charge the troops guarding it: there would probably be
shooting and our offices might be hit by stray bullets (they
were). It was not our quarrel and they did not want any of
us hurt. We could do no proper work in the circumstances
and there was therefore no point in our remaining in the
building. Would we be so kind as to return to our houses
until the trouble was over?

We protested that what they proposed was suicidal: the
troops were bound to open fire and many of the unarmed
demonstrators would be killed. Our visitor replied that this
was a risk which had to be accepted: only a dramatic move
would concentrate the minds of the politicians. After some
more discussion we agreed to evacuate our offices. We came
downstairs, to find that the demonstrators had formed a
cordon through which we had to pass: for some unknown
reason they clapped us as we walked through, girl secretaries, clerks, wireless operators, diplomats, with the Ambassador bringing up the rear. As we walked round the building
to our cars, which were parked in a side street at the back,
we heard the chanting start up again: as we drove away we
heard gunfire. Many brave men died that afternoon but the

stratagem worked. The next day a provisional government was formed comprising all the political parties under the chairmanship of Sirr el Khatim el Khalifa, a distinguished and popular educationalist and academic.

An uneasy calm descended on the city, the first rapture dampened by the incident outside the Palace. There was worse to come. Tension was rising amongst the southerners in Khartoum. Some weeks after the formation of the provisional government, a southern Minister flew to the troubled areas on a mission of conciliation. On the day of his return a rumour circulated that his aircraft had been forced down by the military and that he had been arrested. (In fact his aircraft had been obliged to land at an intermediate airfield because of bad weather.) The southerners in Khartoum exploded. My wife and I were made forcibly aware of this in the late afternoon: we were driving down the main avenue when a stone suddenly clanged against the side of the car. We looked round and realised that we were under fire from a group of enormous southerners on the pavement. We dodged down a side street only to be cut off by another fusillade of stones. We could not get back to our house and began a circuitous tour of the city. Soon we could see palls of smoke rising from burning cars and buildings. Eventually we reached the Ambassador's house where I reported what I had seen. We took refuge until late in the evening by which time the city had quietened down. We drove home through streets littered with stones and burnt-out cars, a depressing sight. Shops had been broken into and looted and there were drunken groups of Africans roaming the streets. Our southern cook had disappeared: he returned a day or two later considerably the worse for wear. The question of where he had been was tactfully avoided.

In the morning battle was resumed and we could see from our office windows running fights in progress between southern construction workers and the police and soldiers. It was a scene reminiscent of a past century. The security forces were mainly using tear gas while the tall, athletic construction workers were discharging volleys of steel reinforcement rods which they were using as spears. It could have been the Zulu War. Order was gradually restored and the now returned Minister broadcast an appeal for calm. Heaven knows how many people on both sides died during what was unquestionably the worst day and night of the revolution; for some time afterwards stories were coming in of corpses found floating in the Nile.

Britain was now faced with a difficult decision. President Abboud had paid a State visit to the United Kingdom in the summer of 1964. He had invited the Queen and the Duke of Edinburgh to make a return visit to the Sudan and it had been arranged that the Queen would come early in 1965 following an already planned visit to Ethiopia (still ruled by the Emperor Haile Selassie). The provisional government quickly confirmed the invitation extended by their predecessors. The original invitation had been issued reciprocally by a friendly government with which Britain had close relations. The new regime was an unknown quantity in terms of its foreign policy – it was bound to be more radical and non-aligned than that of General Abboud – and the country was unsettled. But how could we reasonably refuse an invitation from a government which was publicly committed to a return to democratic rule, when an invitation from a military regime had been accepted? The Ambassador's recommendation was that the visit should go ahead, and it was so decided.

Being Head of Chancery, I was kept very busy over the next two or three months with the preparations for the Queen's visit. This gave me an excellent opportunity not just to work closely with the Ministers and officials of the new government, but also to visit the provincial centres which were to be on the Queen's itinerary. It was manifest that the revolutionary government was resolved to make the visit an outstanding event and we had no doubt that the Queen and the Duke of Edinburgh would be received with great affection and regard, not only by the hierarchy of government, but by the Sudanese people as a whole. However, as the date in February arranged for the visit approached, the internal situation took a marked turn for the worse. The provisional government was hanging together by a thread and the followers of the main political factions were beginning to square up to each other.

While the Queen was next door in Ethiopia, street fighting erupted in Khartoum between Communists and Ansar. A decision had to be made, with little time left, whether or not the visit to the Sudan should go ahead. Many members of the British community favoured cancellation purely on grounds of security. In the event, with only about thirty-six hours to go, the Ambassador called on the government. He outlined our anxieties in plain language and declared that he would be obliged to recommend against the visit taking place unless it could be guaranteed that the atmosphere would be peaceful. He proposed that each and all the leaders of the warring factions should broadcast on the radio to their followers calling on them to compose their differences for the duration of the visit and combine to make it a success. This was done and peace descended again on Khartoum.

The visit itself was a triumph. The government exerted every effort to ensure that the administrative arrangements went smoothly – there was a great deal of incredible last-minute improvisation – and the Queen and the Duke were greeted everywhere by massive and enthusiastic crowds. It was the first time I had been involved with a State visit and had been impressed by the meticulousness of the organisation, down to the last detail, demanded by Buckingham Palace. I was even more impressed by the way in which the Queen conducted herself during what must have been a tiring and indeed uncertain time. She was superb. No untoward incidents marred the occasion. One particular scene remains in my mind. The Queen was scheduled to visit Omdurman. As the Royal motorcade drove slowly through the streets, I noticed that, on each side of the road for several miles, at intervals of about twenty yards, were standing members of the Ansar movement, dressed in the short, patched tunics which had been the uniform of the Mahdist armies, silent, with bowed heads, and hands resting on the muzzles of reversed rifles. This was a truly dramatic spectacle, expressive of respect for the Queen, and remembrance of battles and glories long past and, for their adversaries of today, of their current power.

At the conclusion of the State visit we braced ourselves

for a resumption of the conflict in the streets. But it did not come. Somehow the brief lull and the celebratory aura which had surrounded the visit had cooled the martial ardour of the contestants and relative calm prevailed for the six months remaining of my tour of duty in the Sudan.

Our life resumed its interrupted routine of work and leisure. With a difference: notwithstanding the turbulence which lay close beneath the surface and the host of unsolved and apparently insoluble problems confronting the Sudan, the spirit of liberation which had attended the revolution persisted. Khartoum became livelier, more dynamic, more colourful. Our circle of Sudanese friends and acquaintances widened rapidly and we spent many an animated evening discussing the problems of the country, the policies of our own government and the nature of Sudanese society. One of the favourite topics of debate was whether the Sudanese regarded themselves as Arabs or as Africans. They were Muslim and Arabic was their native language: they felt strongly and emotionally about the crises of the Arab world, particularly Palestine. But their relationship with their great northern neighbour, Egypt, was heavy with historical complexities. The unity of the Nile Valley had been a powerful rallying cry under the Egyptian monarchy and King Farouk had to the end styled himself as King of Egypt and the Sudan. He had in fact, under the condominium, been the titular sovereign of successive British Governors-General. Egypt had loomed over the Sudan as an imperial or quasi-imperial power for over 130 years and, in the last days, Egyptian acquiescence in Sudanese independence had been achieved only after difficult negotiation. There were still many ties between Egyptians and Sudanese.

At the same time, Sudan was fiercely proud of her independence and my Sudanese interlocutors felt deeply involved with Black Africa, now rapidly acquiring independence after a century or more, much longer in the case of the Portuguese, of European imperialism. I sometimes felt that the emotions of my Sudanese acquaintances were more deeply stirred by the troubles in the Congo, the travails of Rhodesia, the continuation of apartheid in South Africa, the fortunes of the former British East African territories, than they were by the more remote rumblings of the Arab world. And yet again ... the debate had no clear outcome.

Once more the time had come for us to move on. I was informed by the Foreign Office that I had been appointed Political Agent in Bahrain. This would be a change. In Egypt and in the Sudan I had lived and worked in a climate of republicanism, of the casting-off of the shackles of an earlier age, of non-alignment in foreign policy, of Arab socialism, of revolution. Now I was to move back in time to serve in a small, monarchical state, ruled in the traditional Arab manner, still under British protection, with Britain responsible for the foreign policy and external defence of the shaikhdom. A great contrast lay ahead of me and there was much discussion of how I would fare. By this time the Scotts had left and our new Ambassador and his wife were John and Diana Richmond, until recently in Kuwait. They had much to tell me about life and work in the Gulf to offset the stream of jokes about my 'imperialist' future, which flowed from my Sudanese friends.

At the close of every chapter of this book, I have written of the sadness of leaving a country and parting from friends of all nationalities. This is the dark side of diplomatic life, compensated for by the excitement of never knowing until the last minute what fresh adventure lies ahead. So it was with the Sudan. We had packed a great deal into our short stay. We had experienced yet another unique and fascinating country and would carry away with us vivid memories. We had been present at a series of events almost without precedent in modern history, certainly in the history of the Arab world. We had made many friends whom we would sadly miss and we would not be present to witness what the immediate future would bring. But still an unknown and intriguing future of our own lay ahead and we relaxed happily in the Scotts' house near Dartmouth while we prepared ourselves for our next assignment.

Twenty years later

It is now twenty years since I left the Sudan and I have not been back. However, I have followed closely the fortunes of the country and of its tough, brave and forthright people. I wish that I could tell a story of success but I cannot. The excitement and hope generated by the overthrow of the military government in September 1964 soon lapsed into political factionalism and economic stagnation. In 1969, the same year in which Colonel Qaddafi seized power in Libya, the Sudanese Army moved in again and military rule was resumed under President Ja'afar Numeiri. At first, as in 1958, the restoration of tranquillity was greeted with relief and Numeiri vastly enhanced his prestige by settling the rebellion in the South in 1972. For a brief period in the 1970s it looked as though Arab oil money might enable the Sudan to realise the economic potential of its vast territories, at present irrigated only by sparse and sporadic rainfall. But the last seven or eight years have witnessed a sad relapse. The economic miracle failed to happen and the civil war in the South resumed. President Numeiri's rule became increasingly dictatorial and the imposition of strict Islamic legislation disturbed the majority of northerners, while totally alienating the non-Muslim South. In 1985 Numeiri suffered the fate of General Abboud, again as a result of a national strike. At the time of writing (autumn 1985) another military group rules provisionally with no permanent political accommodation in prospect. Meanwhile the economy has declined to crisis point with the lethal droughts which have plagued the Horn of Africa creating inward flows of starving Ethiopian refugees into the Sudan and outward flows of famine-stricken Sudanese into the neighbouring states to the west.

What has gone wrong in the Sudan in the thirty years of its independence? Why is it that the Sudanese people, so admired by their British colleagues and former enemies for seventy years or so, and possessing in full the gamut of military and administrative virtues, have failed to achieve a stable political structure? It is not that the Sudanese are by nature excitable and ungovernable. Yes, they are individualistic and impatient of dictatorship. But they are imbued with a deep vein of common sense (British style), humour (also British style) and they are, generally speaking, slow to move to passion. They should have been, as expected by their British mentors, the standard-bearers of parliamentary democracy in Africa. In practice the country has lurched unsteadily from political confusion to military rule and back again although, until recently, the latter was a great deal more benign than most, given the excesses of military regimes elsewhere in the world.

Many reasons can be advanced but none of them – not even all of them added together – can provide a full answer to these questions. The division of the country between the Arabic-speaking Muslim North and the Christian/animist tribal South has greatly complicated the task of successive Sudanese governments. But it was not insoluble, as President Numeiri proved in 1972. The division of the North between those who have traditionally looked towards Egypt for their inspiration and those who are supporters of the Mahdist movement is another cause. And yet, the present leaders of both groupings are intelligent, patriotic and reasonable men who should be capable of sinking their differences in the interest of the good government of the Sudan as a whole. The great size and diversity of the country is another contributory issue but it is nothing to the similar problems of, say, India, while the river Nile which traverses the country from south to north should be something of a unifying factor.

Perhaps the answer lies in the economy. Basically the Sudan has only two natural resources, namely land to the extent of the whole of Western Europe and the Nile. Had these two resources been developed in combination on a large scale, the Sudan could have become one of the richest countries in Africa, producing cash crops such as cotton and sugar and food sources such as cattle and cereals in quantities far beyond the needs of the comparatively small population. But this has not happened for reasons of lack of the necessary capital investment: the Sudan has no source of foreign exchange, such as oil, to generate the capital required, nor any attractions, in its present state, to offer to overseas investors. Hence the country has stumbled along, heavily dependent on foreign aid (a substantial quantity having come, I am glad to say, from Britain) and on the vagaries of the economic policies of successive governments which have desperately tried to make bricks without an adequate supply of straw. The result has been a permanent condition of malaise. As the other Arab countries have got richer, thus enhancing the expectations of the Sudanese people, disillusionment with government has become endemic; all political parties have felt that they could do better than whoever is in power at the moment or has been in the past. There has been no central and universally accepted theme of economic and social development on which to found a national consensus. 'We cannot be worse off than we are now, so any change must be for the better' is the philosophy which has perhaps set party against party and even temporarily united warring elements in opposition to the government of the day. When added to the inherent political and ethnic divisions of the Sudan, this central and apparently permanent economic crisis may well have precipitated the morass in which the country has become mired and which it so ill deserves.

FIVE

Bahrain

By the 1960s the sun was setting on the long history of Britain's peculiar relationship with the small Arab states on the southern shore of the Persian Gulf. Over a period of more than a century Britain had concluded a series of treaties with the rulers of these states. The details of these agreements varied from state to state but, from the beginning of the century, the features common to all were independence in internal affairs with the British government bearing responsibility for the conduct of their foreign relations and external defence. This system had worked to the benefit of both sides: the British had enjoyed secure communications to and from the Indian Empire, and the integrity of the shaikhdoms had been maintained against the ambitions of the Ottoman Empire, the European powers, and contending forces within the Arabian peninsula.

By the late 1940s cracks were beginning to appear in the carapace of isolation which British protection had thrown over the Gulf. Oil had been discovered, first in Bahrain in the early 1930s and latterly in Kuwait. The British interest in imperial communications had declined with the independence of the Indian subcontinent and the shaikhdoms had begun to feel the impact of Arab nationalism and its problems, particularly Palestine. However, the shaikhdoms were small and defenceless, while the growing importance to Britain of Arab oil, particularly after the Abadan crisis in Iran in the early 1950s, plus major residual responsibilities in the Far East, provided fresh reasons for maintaining a connexion which now seemed increasingly archaic to the outside world.

The convulsions of the 1950s in the Arab world – the Arab/Israeli conflicts, the rise of Nasserism, the Suez affair and the revolution in Iraq – sent waves of shock through the small states which had hitherto been immune to such currents. In Bahrain, in particular, there were serious disturbances which temporarily jeopardised stability but, by the end of the decade, tranquillity had returned to the area.

In 1961, Kuwait, whose ties with Britain were looser and more recent than those of the others, terminated the treaties and became fully independent. I have already told in Chapter Three the story of the threat which followed from Iraq and of the measures taken by Britain to counter it. The denouement of this incident was the replacement of British troops by a multilateral force from the Arab League and the eventual acceptance by Iraq of Kuwaiti independence and membership of the League and of the United Nations. However, in case of further need, the British government maintained a military headquarters in Bahrain plus an infantry battalion, additional to the Air Force and Naval bases already situated there. The government of Bahrain showed no disposition to end the protective relationship with Britain. Apart from other reasons, successive Iranian Shahs had claimed the islands since the eighteenth century, and all diplomatic attempts to solve this dispute had failed. Bahrain could ill afford to exchange the protection of a major European power against its huge neighbour for the prestige of defenceless independence: it was common knowledge that the Iranians had gone so far as to designate Bahrain as the 14th province of Iran and that two Deputies, allegedly representing Bahrain, sat in the parliament in Tehran. The claim was no idle threat.

Britain's diplomatic deployment in the Gulf was a direct legacy of the Indian Political Service. A Political Resident, shades of the Indian 'Native States', had his headquarters in Bahrain and was responsible for supervising the conduct of our relations with the protected states as a whole, as well as being Commander-in-Chief of the British-officered but locally raised Trucial Oman Scouts, the 'Army' of the seven small shaikhdoms on the southern shore of the Gulf (now the United Arab Emirates). Then there were Political Agents in Bahrain, Qatar, Dubai and Abu Dhabi, and a Consul-General in Oman. These officials were subordinate to the Political Resident and were in effect mini-Ambassadors to the states to which they were accredited, as well as being the advisers of the Rulers on foreign affairs and external defence. These were unique and unfamiliar posts for the run-of-the-mill British diplomat.

So this was the scene into which I was about to be projected in 1965. I had never served in the Gulf before but I was familiar with it from my wartime service and from my tour in the Embassy in Baghdad. I had also spent a time in the 1950s in the old Eastern Department of the Foreign Office dealing with Gulf affairs. However, I had in the previous ten years become accustomed to situations in the Arab world, particularly in Egypt and the Sudan and to some extent in Jordan, where it had been our policy to create new relationships free of the trammels of the past, indeed to make clear that the future would be founded on equality rather than historical influence. Now I was to play a part in the perpetuation (for the indefinite future so far as I could judge) of a state of affairs which was already under heavy fire from those Arab revolutionary quarters whose aspirations I had observed at close hand, and which was a far cry from the republican, socialist, non-aligned pretensions of Nasserism – in short, a last corner of the glacis of a now defunct imperial system.

I would also be experiencing a wholly different form of Arab government. I had seen the simulacrum of constitutional monarchy at work in Iraq, the struggle to sustain genuine democracy in Turkey, the personal rule of the Hashemite King of Jordan, military government and revolution in Egypt and the Sudan respectively. Now I would be working closely with a regime cast in the traditional Arab mould, which had not changed in fundamentals since the Al Khalifah family, aristocrats from one of the great tribal confederations of the Arabian peninsula, had conquered the islands of Bahrain in the late eighteenth century.

Would I be able to make the necessary intellectual adjustments to cope adequately with this novel situation? Would I get on with the Ruler, Shaikh Isa bin Sulman al Khalifah, who had come to the throne on the death of his father less than four years before? Could I work with the

Political Resident, Sir William Luce, a distinguished former official of the Sudan Political Service and an ex-Governor of Aden? Was I, with my recent experience and personal sympathies, the right person to play a quasi-imperial role which I could not help regarding with some disfavour as an anachronism in a world in which decolonisation had become a guiding beacon? All these questions and more bothered my wife and myself as I set about my preliminary briefing.

As the day of our departure drew near, one of the questions in my mind resolved itself to my complete satisfaction. Sir William and Lady Luce were in England on leave. They invited me to tea at their house in Hampshire, in order, I suppose, to see what I was like: we had never met before. My wife, who was again pregnant and looking after our two boys, did not accompany me; and I set out from Devonshire in a slightly prickly mood, assuring my wife that I would speak my mind. First, I picked up my daughter, now ten years old, from Bedales, and took her with me to the Luces. I anticipated a difficult passage with a man whose record suggested that he would be the embodiment of the past which, in my small way, I had spent so much time and effort in trying to bury. I returned to Dartmouth in a different frame of mind, a devotee of Sir William with whom I remained on terms of close friendship until his sudden and premature death twelve years later. Progressive, cultured, humane and humorous, Sir William was a man who immediately commanded the admiration and respect of everyone whom he met, myself included. I had always been fortunate in my superiors in the Diplomatic Service and I had struck lucky again. That evening I confessed to my wife that I was now a confirmed member of the Luce fan club and that she need have no anxieties about our ability to get on with our new boss and his wife (I hope that Lady Luce, if she reads these lines, will appreciate the magic which she and her husband worked).

I cannot say that the political climate was equally reassuring. The Cairo propaganda machine had targeted British imperialism and its stooges in the Gulf as priority objectives and, elsewhere in the Arabian peninsula, British policy was under stern attack: the South Arabian Federation, constructed a few years previously to provide a framework for the eventual independence of Aden and the Aden Protectorates, was fighting a losing battle against external subversion (Cairo again) and internal opposition. More important, political pressure was beginning to mount in Britain itself for withdrawal from our 'East of Suez' commitments, including the Gulf. In 1963, Britain's first attempt to join the European Economic Community had been blocked by President de Gaulle's veto. A public debate about Britain's role in the world had followed this setback and the advent of a Labour government in 1964 after thirteen years of Conservative rule had strengthened the hand of those who believed that, for both financial and political reasons, Britain should without delay shed the final trappings of Empire: Europe yes, if the French veto could be overcome; the Atlantic Alliance certainly; the Commonwealth probably, for reasons of sentiment; but not old-fashioned commitments to old-fashioned Arabs in the teeth of the hostility of the 'progressive' forces in the region. A question was being more insistently asked – were overseas military bases factors for stability or magnets for opposition? Were British soldiers not being needlessly exposed to risk when their very presence was creating the turbulence which made it impossible for them to carry out their tasks? If we dismantled the communications system which still stretched from Britain to Singapore and beyond, the bases could be withdrawn, the local governments would be freed of an incubus which had progressively alienated them from their own people, the British taxpayer would save money and a casus belli between Britain and the newly independent Third World would have disappeared. So the argument ran. It had not as yet influenced government policy, but the Gulf rulers were uneasily conscious that the foundation on which their world had rested for so long was beginning to tremble. In addition, in Bahrain itself, there had been rioting in the summer of 1965, caused principally by agitation within the labour force, and the resources of the government had been stretched to the limit to maintain control of security. Hence, although everything on the surface was peaceful enough as our aircraft landed at Muharraq Airport in the late summer

5 Anthony and Sheila Parsons being presented to the Queen on
a State visit to the Sudan, 1965

6 The Ruler of Bahrain, Shaikh Isa bin Sulman al Khalifah,
and Anthony Parsons, 1966

7 The Parsons in the garden of their home in Bahrain, 1965

8 Anthony Parsons tape-recording the annual manumission celebrations by descendants of slaves at the Political Agency, Bahrain, 1967

of 1965, there was plenty of potential trouble in the background, in Bahrain itself, in the Arabian peninsula, in the attitude of the revolutionary Arab governments, and in the rumblings of dissent about our Gulf policy coming from elements in the British political establishment. The next few years looked likely to be if anything too stimulating: there was certainly no danger of boredom.

For once we had travelled in undisturbed comfort. Coming up in the world, we were entitled to first-class fares; the children were at school and this time we were not burdened with cat baskets and litter trays – the brute was being cared for by our successors in Khartoum to be airfreighted to Bahrain after we had settled in. We were met at the airport by the British, Indian and Bahraini staff of the Political Agency and their wives plus a representative of the Bahrain government, the Ruler's first cousin Shaikh Mohammed bin Mubarak, now one of the longest serving Foreign Ministers in the Arab World. Shaikh Mohammed bin Mubarak, young, lively and Oxford-educated, was to become a close personal friend: I realised, after five minutes' conversation in the small and cosy V.I.P. lounge, that, if all Bahrainis were like him, my stay would be agreeable, and that there would be no lack of the kind of animated conversation to which I had become accustomed in other Arab capitals.

Our formal welcome complete, we were driven across the narrow causeway which separated Muharraq Island from the capital, Manama, and were deposited at the Political Agency, destined to be our home for nearly four years, the longest period I had spent in one place since I was born, with the exception of our posting in Turkey.

The Bahrain Agency, now the Embassy, was a triumph of Ministry of Works design and construction. The old building had collapsed some years before, almost on the head of the then Political Agent as he was eating his breakfast, and the new Agency had been built on the same spot. In our time, land reclamation was in its infancy and the shallow waters of the Gulf lapped up to within a few feet of the house. The garden was large and old with huge trees, in particular an immense banyan with spreading convoluted roots around which certain members of the Indian community gathered on feast days. A far-sighted predecessor had installed a clay tennis court at the bottom of the garden and an ample irrigation tank served as a swimming pool. The water in the pool was fresh but, for some unexplained reason, the level rose and fell a few feet daily with the tide beyond the wall; oleanders formed a canopy over the pool, welcome shade for the swimmers.

The building itself combined offices on the ground floor with our living quarters on the first and second storey. Central air-conditioning provided a cool and dry contrast to the sweltering heat outside the seaward-looking windows which ran along two sides of the enormous combined drawing-room and dining-room, divided when necessary by sliding doors. Downstairs the Agent's suite of offices was separated from the other sections of the Mission, political, commercial and consular. At the east end was another house, the Agency Court.

Here was another strange feature of the British relationship with the Gulf states. Because of the original absence of legislation, apart from the Islamic Sharia courts, the Ruler of Bahrain, years previously, had ceded to Britain jurisdiction over all non-Muslim foreigners. Two British judges, based on the Political Residency, dispensed justice from the Agency Court in Bahrain, and its equivalents in other Gulf states, according to a mixture of British common law and legislation deriving from the days of the Indian Empire. Americans, Europeans, Indians, sailors of all nationalities, were dealt with on criminal and civil offences by the Agency Court. A by-product of this curious jurisdictional arrangement was the issue of liquor permits. Drink was formally outlawed for the Bahrainis and liquor permits were issued by the Political Agent to those who came under our jurisdiction. The concessions for the import and sale of drink were originally confined to two British companies in Bahrain, although a leading firm of Bahraini merchants had recently succeeded in breaking this monopoly. The Agent's power to dispense or withhold these priceless permits made him a man worth cultivating by the foreign community!

Before returning to my main narrative, I should mention another interesting relic of bygone days – the manumission of slaves. Slavery had been abolished in Bahrain a century before but the Political Agent still had the power of issuing certificates of manumission. A pile of these documents mouldered in a cupboard in my office. On three occasions during my tour of duty I was visited by men of African origin from the Arabian mainland who claimed that they were ex-slaves whom their former masters – none of them Bahrainis – were trying to repossess. They demanded certificates, which I gave them with fitting solemnity. On one such occasion the alleged slave-owner, a small merchant, came to the Agency, presumably to recover his property. I called him to my office in the company of the gentleman to whom I had just given the certificate of manumission, having first taken the precaution of spreading a large Union Jack over my desk. I showed the merchant – I will not disclose his nationality – the newly signed certificate and informed him in awful tones that, if he continued to pursue the liberated man, I could assure him that the full wrath of Her Britannic Majesty would descend on his head. He looked suitably apprehensive and gave me the necessary assurance. The two of them departed, amicable relations apparently restored, and I saw them no more.

Still on the subject of slavery, another touching tradition was maintained at the Agency, through no prompting of our own. In the distant past, if a slave wished to be freed and was being pursued by his or her owner, he or she had only to reach and clasp the high flagpole in the Agency garden for the pursuit to be abandoned. This sporting preliminary to the manumission procedure was commemorated down to the time of which I write by the descendants of slaves in the islands. Every New Year's Day, in the morning, a party of these people, male and female, would congregate at the flagpole and entertain us and interested passers-by to a few hours of dancing, music and singing, African style. The men wore skirts of sharks' teeth which rattled rhythmically like castanets as they danced; the instruments, the songs and dances were those of East Africa, not Arabia. It was a strange outlandish scene, enacted by people who had by this time been Arabic-speaking Muslims for generations. Unfortunately my amateurish tape-record-

111

ings of this ceremony have long since worn out through over-use.

On the evening of our arrival at the Agency, our influential driver, Sayyid Amin, showed us into the house and introduced us to our staff of efficient and admirable Goanese servants. He explained to us the origin of the sedan chair in the hall – Lord Curzon had been carried ashore on it from a British warship on his visit to Bahrain in 1903 – and left us to explore our new home. We did so with delight and went to bed in high spirits. Many of the doubts which had plagued me in my briefing period had dissipated in my first hours in Bahrain.

We woke early and wandered in the garden, exchanging greetings and conversation with the four old Shia villagers who worked there. We had heard the humidity pouring off the roof like rain in the night and there were puddles of water in the paved courtyard. The enervating, damp heat of the day had yet to come and the sky was soft, opalescent. There was no breath of wind and the surface of the sea was like clouded glass, pale green, punctuated by arrow-shaped fish traps. The air was heavy with that unmistakable smell of the Gulf, a mingling of salt, mud, coral, fish and heaven knows what else. Dhows, powered by diesel engines, chugged along far offshore; the sea was so shallow that you could walk out a mile or more without having to swim. The brief suspension of time passed; the Agency staff began to arrive for the day's work and I was off.

My first call was on the Ruler, Shaikh Isa, who received me in his small and unpretentious palace at Rifa'a, twenty minutes' drive in the country south of Manama. As the car rushed along, my driver pointed out the sights – the compound at Jufair housing the Political Residency, the Naval headquarters and the small American Naval presence. Then there was the Virgin's Pool, already full of splashing Bahraini children, of great depth and the home of fabulously sized fish. We left the palm groves on the outskirts of the town and headed into the desert. On the right rose the high kilns of the pottery village of Aali where, I was told, the method of making cooking utensils and other objects had not changed for three thousand years. On our left we passed through a half-built estate of low-cost houses of varying sizes, each with its walled courtyard. This was Isa Town, being built by a British firm, eventually to accommodate, on easy terms, thousands of Bahraini families.

We arrived at the Palace. I had been warned that I would be confronted by a Guard of Honour of the Bahraini State Police whose salute I must acknowledge before greeting the Ruler. I had been advised to wear a hat so that I could respond appropriately to the 'present arms'. I had decided against this concession to formality. I had not worn a hat since I had left the Army years before and my decision was made easy by the fact that I did not possess one. I inclined my head respectfully as the Guard presented arms, and then walked forward to shake hands with the Ruler. We entered his Majlis (Council Chamber) and sat down side by side at the end of a long room. Bitter coffee and orange juice followed in quick succession and I was relieved to find that His Highness, like me, was a heavy smoker: there would be no embarrassment about lighting up.

I had noticed on entering the Palace courtyard that there was a number of men standing around with peregrine falcons perched on their wrists: well-bred saluki dogs lay about on the sand. Altogether a picturesque sight. I was not however prepared for a close encounter with one of these formidable birds. From time to time during our conversation the Ruler would summon one of his retainers to give him instructions. The man knelt down close to Shaikh Isa in order to conduct the conversation sotto voce, a falcon on his wrist. I suddenly realised that its fierce eyes were fixed on mine at a range of about six inches. The bird's demeanour was far from welcoming and I kept very still until the danger had passed. It took me a week or two to become accustomed to this accompaniment to my meetings with the Ruler.

When I left the Palace about half an hour later after the ceremony of rose-water and incense which, in Bahrain, tactfully indicates that the time for departure has arrived, another of my doubts had been well and truly laid to rest. Shaikh Isa could not have been more friendly and welcoming. With the perfect manners common to all his family,

113

he put me quickly at my ease. On this first call we did not discuss important subjects but there was no mistaking his shrewdness and the extent of his knowledge of everything that was going on in his country. To my great relief he was utterly lacking in solemnity and the glint of humour never left his eyes. I realised that any demonstration of pomposity or imperial remoteness on my part would be dissolved by laughter. I returned to the Agency to report to my wife that, as I saw it – I could not of course speak for Shaikh Isa – I had just met a man with whom it would be a pleasure to do business.

I spent the following weeks getting to know my job and familiarising myself with Bahrain. I called on the numerous relations of the Ruler, uncles, great-uncles and cousins, and on the officials of the government with whom I would be working. I met the leaders of the large British community, of the British Armed Services, the chief Bahraini merchants, Indians, Pakistanis, American oil company executives and so on and so on. I travelled all over the islands. There was no lack of variety.

At the end of this initial period I was beginning to understand some of the complexities confronting Bahrain. The main island was small, only thirty miles long and about ten miles wide; much of it was desert, and agriculture, which had flourished along the northern coastline in early days, had declined. The population of 250,000 was mainly urban and increasing rapidly with the steady fall in infant mortality and the greater life expectancy resulting from thirty years or more of free medical services: endemic diseases such as malaria had been eliminated. Universal free education up to secondary level over the same period had produced a literate, politically conscious, younger generation, many of whom had studied at universities in Cairo, Beirut and Baghdad. This blend of youth and political awareness was compounded by the division, more or less in equal proportions, of the population into adherents of the Shia sect (the indigenous people of the towns and villages) and the Sunni sect (who had followed the Al Khalifah from the mainland in the nineteenth century). The two communities traditionally regarded each other with mutual dislike, and serious clashes between them had not been infrequent in the recent past. Broadly speaking the Sunnis found their inspiration in Nasser's Cairo, the Shia in revolutionary Iraq.

Paradoxically these sophisticated people, a microcosm of the most advanced societies in the Arab world, were ruled in the old-fashioned patriarchal style of tribal Arab government. There were no representative institutions. Shaikh Isa and his two brothers, Shaikh Khalifah the head of Administration and Shaikh Mohammed the head of Police and Security, formed the apex of a pyramid which descended to a series of functional Departments (there were no Ministers as such) dealing with such matters as Finance, Education, Development, Communications, Ports, Agriculture, Oil Affairs and so on. Some of these Departments were headed by members of the Ruling Family, others by Bahraini technocrats, both Sunni and Shia. In addition, this apparently incongruous superstructure was in an antiquated relationship with the British, the favourite whipping boys of the radio stations of Cairo, Baghdad and Damascus to which the bulk of the population seemed to be permanently glued.

Furthermore the Bahrain government was in no position, as was the case elsewhere in the Gulf, to allay political dissidence by the lavish distribution of money. Bahrain was the first of the Gulf states, indeed of all the states in the Arabian peninsula, where oil had been discovered in the early 1930s. But the quantity was small and, by the 1960s, most of the oil which was fed into the Sitra refinery in the south of the main island was piped from Saudi Arabia. Bahrain was a trading community with three thousand years of mercantile tradition behind it, rather than an 'oil shaikhdom'. The domestic market was too small to absorb major industrial expansion and historically many of the jobs in the active private sector – banking, insurance, import/export, retail services, etc. – were held by foreigners, mainly British, Indians and Pakistanis. Investment and the location of regional enterprises in Bahrain were handicapped by the fact that the Iranian government made difficulties about dealing with any foreign concern which made Bahrain its headquarters. The pearling industry, which had been Bahrain's principal source of wealth in pre-oil days, had been destroyed by Japanese competition in the 1920s and 1930s. For all these reasons there was imminent danger of unemployment amongst the rapidly growing Bahraini population, their expectations roused by education and their political aspirations excited by events elsewhere in the region.

I have outlined a classical revolutionary situation. And yet, apart from the labour troubles of the summer of 1965, the island had been peaceful since the subsidence of the pan-Arab spring tides of the 1950s. There were, as I saw it as my knowledge of Bahrain increased, both external and internal reasons for this remarkable state of affairs. The Iranian claim hung heavily over the island and even the most ardent revolutionaries realised that, were the British to be forced out as appeared to be happening in Aden, there was more than a possibility that the Shah would attempt to seize Bahrain by force. This would certainly bring Saudi Arabia to Bahrain's defence. Hence those who aspired to fill the vacuum left by the British withdrawal might find that they had inherited a battlefield from which either Iran or Saudi Arabia, not themselves, would emerge victorious. This was a deterrent to pushing political dissension beyond certain limits.

More important, however, were the factors for stability inherent in the nature of the regime. General elections, parliaments, constitutions might be absent but where were these mechanisms genuinely operative in the rest of the Arab world? In their place there was a system under which, in the circumstances of a small and compact community, the aspirations and the grievances of the people could be expressed more effectively than in the Western or Eastern European adaptations of Cairo or Baghdad, let alone under military dictatorship. The Ruler sat in open Council two or three times a day for seven days in every week. Any man in the island had the right to walk into these sessions and address himself direct to his Head of State. Yes, the Ruler had the last word but this process not only provided him with an awareness of what was pleasing or worrying his people far keener than any bureaucratic system could have supplied. It also provided the people with an outlet for their views and a sense of accessibility to the source of decision making, which the most democratic system in a large and more diffused geopolitical entity could not hope to emulate.

This tradition of maintaining open Majlis was followed by the senior members of the Ruling Family, thus disseminating this direct contact between rulers and ruled at different levels. This modus operandi, informal and unsystematised, created an atmosphere of cosiness in which the jagged edges of opposition were smoothed away. I have seen men, virulent in their opposition to the regime and in some cases recently released from terms of imprisonment for subversive activity, deep in conversation with Shaikh Isa in his Majlis and departing, with a specific grievance satisfied, in an amicable frame of mind. The grounds of their opposition might remain but the bitterness had been blunted.

This extension to a modern, urbanised society of a form of rule originating in the nomadic, pastoral and rural world of the Arabian peninsula owed little or nothing to a century and a half of British influence. It was in day-to-day administration rather than politics that traces of the British hand could be discovered. In the 1920s, Shaikh Hamad, the grandfather of the present Ruler, had recruited, at the suggestion of the British government, an Adviser, Charles (later Sir Charles) Belgrave, to help with the modernisation of an apparatus which had become too primitive to cope with the demands of the post-war world. Belgrave stayed in Bahrain for over thirty years and helped to fashion the simple, but effective, structure of functional Departments and semi-detached Municipalities which was in being on my arrival. Most of the departments of government were still housed in one building, the Secretariat, in which the Ruler and his brothers would gather three times a week for the equivalent of Cabinet meetings when officials would be co-opted as necessary. Shaikh Khalifah was, in all but name, the Prime Minister. Forthright, intelligent and practical, his loyalty to his brother was absolute and he made a firm and effective head of the Administration. There was much talent in support. Young, able and western-educated shaikhs were to be found in the police, in the port administration and elsewhere, while some of the senior officials such as Sayyed Mahmoud (Finance) and Yousuf Shirawi (Oil and Development), respectively a Shia and a Sunni, would have made their mark in the Council of Ministers of any state, large or small. In a nutshell the Administration worked, punctually, without corruption and with reasonable efficiency and fairness, another source of stability.

British officials were scattered through the Departments in advisory capacities but, except for the Bahrain State Police (the only armed force available to the government except for a couple of hundred lightly armed Bedouin attached to the Ruler's person), which had a British Commandant plus twenty or thirty British officers, they were few in number and disappearing rapidly to be replaced by Bahrainis.

The notion that Bahrain's independence in internal affairs was more apparent than real and that 'the British' were the real power behind the throne was widespread, not only amongst Bahrainis but also amongst many British observers. The truth was far less sinister. If the Ruler asked us for advice or asked for help in recruiting British personnel, we did our best to be forthcoming. If we detected some development which we thought should be drawn to the attention of the Ruler or his government, for example something which was causing public dissatisfaction, we would do so. But there was no attempt to coerce, no threat of 'or else'. We accepted that Shaikh Isa ran his own show and that his judgement on internal matters was likely to be sounder than ours. Let me give an example. In 1965 we suggested to him that the administrative structure needed reform. We felt that greater opportunities should be given to non-shaikhly Bahrainis and that there were too many ageing, undesirable and incompetent British officials in the police and elsewhere: their presence was politically damaging and their performance no compensation for this liability. Shaikh Isa asked for our views in writing, which I gave him. He pondered on them for some months and discussed them with his advisers. Eventually he made clear to me that he would prefer the matter to be dropped: I did so without argument. Even the deadbeat British officials escaped, Shaikh Isa being too good-natured to upset people

118

who, however useless in the present, had given loyal service in the past.

Another case in point was the Economic Survey. Also in 1965 the Bahrain Government asked the Ministry of Overseas Development for recommendations for a development programme, the main purpose being to absorb the rising unemployment amongst Bahraini school-leavers. Some time later I handed the report to the official in charge of Development, Yousuf Shirawi. I made no secret of the fact that I regarded it as unimaginative, cottage-industry stuff which would be unlikely to relieve the pressures on the economy. I made clear that our task was now complete. We had produced what had been asked for and it was now up to Bahrain to decide what to do. If they wanted further help from us, we were available.

In a wider sense Bahrain was an excellent example of the strength of a Muslim community in resisting alien cultural penetration. Intimacy with Britain dated back over 150 years and English was the second language of the majority. Britain was Bahrain's principal trading partner and most of the foreign commercial enterprises were British. The older generation of Bahrainis, those who had been abroad for their education, had gone to British India, mainly to Bombay, and the younger generation from the well-to-do merchant families were no strangers to London and other British cities. The British community in the 1960s, including about 3000 members of the Armed Services, must have amounted to over 6000, nearly $2\frac{1}{2}$ per cent of the total population. And yet the way of life of the Bahrainis, shaikhs, merchants and people as a whole, went on in a variety of traditional patterns, apparently unaffected by the pressures of foreign influence. It was not that the two sides shunned each other: there was plenty of contact, almost all of it amicable, in the workplace and socially. However, broadly speaking, the communities lived their separate lives, notwithstanding the tiny size of the main island. For political reasons, the British Armed Forces were kept aloof and were forbidden to come into town in uniform except on duty. They maintained this practice with admirable discipline and restraint. The hundreds of British and American officials of the oil company lived mainly in their lavish compound in the south of the island, and the British commercial community occupied residential areas where there were few Bahrainis. The business area of Manama, the capital, was Arab with a sprinkling of Indians: it gave no impression of a city permeated by foreigners, while the second largest town, Muharraq, close to the Royal Air Force base, was untouched by British or any other foreign influence. There was only one bone of social contention at the time of my arrival – the Gymkhana Club. This relic of Anglo-Indian days, as its name suggests, was a Sudan Club in miniature. It had its tennis courts, its swimming pool and its club-house; also, as with its Khartoum counterpart, its exclusive British membership. The Club carried this principle of exclusivity to the length that visiting tennis teams from, for example, the Indian Club (the best players in the island) were not even allowed to take tea or drinks with the home team after a match. I found myself in the embarrassing position of being ex officio patron of both clubs: indeed the Indian Club was one of my favourite resorts for a game of tennis. I also discovered that the attitude of the Gymkhana Club towards the Bahrainis was a source of resentment which had penetrated to the Ruler and his family. I discussed the problem with the Ruler and was able thereafter to tell the Club Committee that, if they did not open their membership to all comers, the future of the Club would be called into question. An Emergency General Meeting of the membership followed. I addressed the gathering at length and a lively exchange of views ensued. At the conclusion, a vote was taken which, unlike the Sudan Club, came down heavily in favour of open membership. The Ruler was invited to become a patron and the lists were opened. As I had expected, very few Bahrainis applied for membership: their secluded family lives precluded mixed tennis, swimming and so on, while the other attractions of the club – the quality of the food and the atmosphere in the public rooms – were less than irresistible. So, with the political odium removed, the British community was able to continue to disport itself according to its own customs: a happy outcome for all concerned.

The long-term future of the protected states of the Gulf was our main strategic preoccupation. The British government had no plans to terminate the existing web of relationships and there was no pressure from the Rulers for us to do so. However, we were conscious that the status quo could not continue indefinitely. The current folklore in Bahrain was that Sir William Luce was determined to dragoon the nine states (the seven Trucial States, Bahrain and Qatar) into a Federation: Oman was recognised as being 'different'. This was not the case. Britain had gained experience of unsuccessful attempts to persuade small regional states into political unions which they had not themselves conceived. The fate of the West Indies Federation and the Federation in South Arabia was fresh in our minds. As I saw it, Bahrain itself did not present a problem. If and when the time came for the termination of the treaties by mutual agreement and Bahrain decided to become a fully independent member of the Arab League and the United Nations, there should be no difficulty on account of size of population, economic base and so on. There were already members of the United Nations smaller than Bahrain. The only obstacle - a big one - would be Bahrain's defencelessness so long as the Iranian claim remained unsettled. Qatar, with its population of well under 100,000, was so close to Saudi Arabia geographically and politically that its future seemed likely to lie in some kind of association with its larger neighbour. Oman, geographically extensive and with a population close to 1 million, could have opted for full independence at any time: internal rebellion and the idiosyncratic character of the then Sultan were the only stumbling blocks. The heart of the problem lay in the seven so-called Trucial States - Dubai, Abu Dhabi, Sharjah, Ras el Khaimah, Ajman, Fujairah and Umm el Qawain. The last three named had microscopic populations of from 2000 to 3000 each; even the larger ones were small compared to Bahrain or Qatar although Abu Dhabi (oil) and Dubai (gold smuggling) were already prosperous. None of them showed signs of wishing to unite with their neighbours and none could on its own sustain full sovereign independence.

Sir William Luce's policy was to encourage all the Rulers

to work together over functional matters such as customs, police, co-ordination of development projects, immigration and the like in the hope that this habit of co-operation might lead to moves towards political co-ordination and eventual organic links, particularly amongst the smaller states. He had no specific ultimate structure in mind. He had been personally involved in the preliminaries to the South Arabian Federation which was clearly falling apart, even before the withdrawal of Britain, in savage rebellion and dissidence. He was not in the mood to launch an analogous experiment in the Gulf. By 1965 a little progress had been made. For the first time on historical record, all the Rulers had met together. Plans for a Gulf currency to replace the Gulf rupee (another British Indian legacy) were afoot, although they were already running into difficulties. Shortly after I arrived the currency plan sank without trace on the rock of the name. Any reference to 'Persian Gulf' on notes or coins would have been unacceptable to the Arabs, while 'Arabian Gulf' or 'Gulf' would have excluded the currency from circulation in Iran: deadlock resulted but the activity generated by the exercise had brought the Finance Department officials of the shaikhdoms closer than they had been before. Furthermore Police Commandants were arranging a meeting and other projects were in gestation. But our hopes of self-generating impetus were low. Most of the states had frontier disputes with each other or deep-seated rivalries which had left a legacy of mutual distrust and dislike. The Iranian factor made some of the smaller states reluctant to co-operate with Bahrain, while those who valued their friendship with Saudi Arabia were chary of too close proximity to Abu Dhabi because of its dispute with the Saudis over the Buraimi oasis. There was no shortage of minefields.

Our domestic life settled quickly into an agreeable routine. Culture was admittedly in short supply: there were no theatres or concerts and the cinemas showed mainly the most lurid of Indian films. Bahrain did not have a television station but the worst of American T.V. was available from the oil company station in Saudi Arabia. Viewing was made more interesting by the puritanical Saudi attitude towards sex and liquor. The cowboy could be seen grasping his glass in the saloon but, hey presto, it was back on the bar again without our having been able to see him in the sinful act of drinking. The hero and heroine moved into an embrace but were suddenly apart without our witnessing the shocking deed of a kiss. Our concentration was, I am sorry to say, riveted more on the hope that the Saudi censor would slip up than on the substance of the programmes. In any case our evenings were too filled with the incessant entertaining characteristic of a small and intimate community to leave room for the distractions of television.

A severe trial to our metabolism was presented by the Ruler's practice, normal in the Gulf, of dining one hour after sunset. His dinner parties were lavish, but short. The guests arrived and coffee was served. Ten minutes later we would dine: the table was always laid for a hundred people and relays from lower down the social scale would take their places when the invited guests had eaten their fill. The custom was to rise from the table and return to the Majlis as soon as you had had enough to eat. After all the guests had reassembled, there was more coffee followed by the ritual incense and rose-water. The whole proceeding lasted about half an hour. This meant that, in winter, we were back at the Agency by about half-past six. It was thus no good using a dinner with the Ruler as an excuse for refusing a dinner party elsewhere. 'But you can come on to us afterwards: there will be plenty of time.' Many was the occasion on which my wife and I ate two dinners in one evening, staggering eventually to bed heavily bloated with food.

In the torrid heat which lasted for seven or eight months of the year we worked a long morning from seven o'clock until two, and spent the rest of the day out of doors, swimming, playing tennis (it was possible to lose half a stone over two sets of singles in the summer), picnicking on the smaller islands in the archipelago and indulging my new passion of ornithology. Bahrain lies on the eastern arm of the migration route from East Africa to Europe and, in spring and autumn, our garden, indeed the whole of the island, was full of migratory birds of all kinds from large sea birds and flamingoes down to a wide variety of garden and moorland birds, wheatears, wrynecks, pipits, shrikes, warblers and so on. My binoculars were always at the ready in my ground-floor office and I spent hours scouring the garden in my bathing trunks identifying new arrivals. Boats were excellent transport for hitch-hiking migrants and I remember causing a sensation on a visiting Indian aircraft carrier. I was paying my formal call on the admiral, dressed in full uniform with sword and decorations, when I saw what I rightly believed to be a rare warbler sitting exhausted under one of the aircraft. With a word of apology to the admiral – we were advancing on the Guard of Honour – I dived under the aircraft to identify the bird at close quarters. The ceremony was suspended until I emerged a minute or two later, my white uniform slightly the worse for wear: my polite hosts continued as if nothing had happened, a little incredulous at my shamefaced explanation of my conduct.

In February 1966, our fourth and last child was born in the Bahrain State Hospital. It was a long but successful ordeal for my wife, now aged forty-three, in the public labour ward, probably the first time a Political Agent's wife had given birth in Bahrain. The weather was cold and rainy and I passed an anxious night in the hospital waiting for my wife to return from the labour ward. We named the baby Laila, a tribute to her birth in Bahrain and to our many years in the Middle East. My wife was overwhelmed with visitors from the lady members of the Ruling Family and our other friends in the Bahraini community. Shaikh Isa himself was away, hawking in Saudi Arabia. The news was transmitted to him and I received a telegram which read 'Congratulations: bad luck'. I took the point. The Shaikh, in the best Arab tradition, had been hoping that we would have another boy and thought it fitting to mingle his compliments with commiseration!

Bahrain, especially the Agency, was a wonderful place for a small baby. In the great old shady garden, Laila first lay in her pram all day long with no clothes on and then, when the time came, staggered around with no clothes on for nine months in the year. My visitors to the office, grave shaikhs, merchants or voluble officials, soon got used to the sight of a small, red-haired, naked figure foraging about outside the french window or hammering on the glass to demand admittance: it was seldom refused. She became an Agency mascot and was atrociously spoilt, which seemed to do her no harm. Presents showered down on her and a monster teddy bear, given to her at her birth by one of the merchants, is still with her now at University. She had a secure and happy life except for the day when she walked into the swimming pool and was fished out just in time. For months afterwards she used to stop and make a detour when she reached the ill-omened spot from which she had plunged in.

Unfortunately I could not devote myself full time to domestic matters. The principal questions on my mind through 1966 were the interlocking problems of the internal political situation and the economy. There had been no outbreaks since the rioting of 1965, but the atmosphere was uneasy. The barrage of Cairo Radio against the British and the shaikhly regimes in the Gulf continued without respite. The impact of this stentorian clamour was compounded by echoes of events in Aden and the Aden Protectorates. The rebellion against the South Arabian Federation was swelling and the British and local authorities there were embattled. The Arab Nationalist Movement and the Arab National Liberation Front were beginning to flex their muscles in Bahrain and a new political banner was flying along the coast of Arabia, the Popular Front for the Liberation of the Arab Gulf. Storm clouds were rolling in our direction. And all was far from well in the Bahrain State Police, the only security force on the island. Rumours were flying in the bazaars of brutality by certain British officers towards 'political' prisoners, both in the prison island of Jida and in the interrogation cells. The truth of these stories was unimportant; as I have suggested elsewhere, it was what people believed to be true that moved events, and everyone believed the rumours. In early 1966 terrorism struck for the first time: two police officers, one British and one Jordanian, were car-bombed. Tension rose and there was much discussion about an Aden situation developing in Bahrain. Shortly afterwards the old Irish Commandant of Police had a bad stroke and had to be flown home, never to return.

The Head of the Special Branch left the island. Shaikh Isa asked us for help in recruiting replacements and we responded quickly. The new Commandant and the new Head of Special Branch, sensitive, skilful and experienced men, settled in. The tension eased without an accompanying wave of repression which would, in that atmosphere, have served only to heighten dissent.

Meanwhile the Development Bureau was wrestling with the associated problem of rising unemployment. The programme submitted the previous year by the British government offered little comfort. Such measures as increased taxation and the establishment of handicrafts and small cottage industries would do little to absorb the thousands of urban school-leavers whose job prospects, or the lack of them, would do much to influence their political frame of mind. The government turned to the American-owned Bahrain Petroleum Company for an alternative Economic Survey. The BAPCO Management, long established in Bahrain and conscious of the link between political stability and the continuing success of their operation, agreed. They tackled the job from a fresh perspective, basing their researches not on the limited size of the domestic market but on Bahrain's central position in communications between the Western world and the Far East and on the existence of large quantities of cheap and unexploited natural gas. By the end of the year their report was beginning to generate optimism. They recommended a whole series of projects in the field of financial and other services: most important from the point of view of employment, they proposed a large aluminium smelter to be based on natural gas from Bahrain with the raw material imported from Australia in empty oil tankers en route to load at Gulf ports, and the finished product being exported around the world. The other major project was a graving dock for supertankers, taking advantage again of Bahrain's cheap energy and geographical position.

Sir William and Lady Luce left on retirement in the summer of 1966 and were replaced by Sir Stewart and Lady Crawford. Sir William's departure was mourned throughout the Gulf by Arabs and British alike. Over the eventful six years during which he had presided over the conduct of

British policy towards the Gulf, he had, perhaps to a greater extent than any of his predecessors, secured the love as well as the respect of the Rulers from Muscat to Bahrain and Qatar: his personal prestige and influence were great. His only disappointment was his failure to promote a greater degree of functional co-operation amongst the small Trucial States. By the end of 1966 the momentum had virtually petered out of this initiative. Sir Stewart had inherited the same problem of the long-term future which had confronted Sir William. But he had also inherited a fund of goodwill and an intimacy with the Arab governments which owed much to the achievements of his predecessor.

New Year's Day in Bahrain had for many years been marked by a ceremony in which the Ruler, accompanied by senior members of his family, called on the Political Resident who was accompanied by the Political Agent. On 1st January 1967 this ceremony took place as usual. Coffee was drunk and light conversation exchanged. After about twenty minutes the guests departed. I doubt if any of us realised how dramatic the year ahead was to prove.

Unlike the other Gulf states, Bahrain was host to only a handful of Palestinians, about forty in all. The majority were working for the government: some occupied senior positions, such as judges in the Bahrain courts. However, the people as a whole were heavily committed emotionally to the cause of Palestine and the government conscientiously maintained the Arab boycott of Israel, even to the extent of banning Elizabeth Taylor's films and confiscating Frank Sinatra's records, both of these worthies having supported Zionism. But the front line was far away and the situation on the ground had been quiet for ten years since Sinai had been demilitarised and occupied by a United Nations peacekeeping force following the Suez affair of 1956. In my first year or so Palestine had been a frequent topic of conversation and argument with my Bahraini interlocutors, but not a major issue.

Now, in the first months of 1967, tension began to rise between Israel and her Arab neighbours. In May the Syrian government (the United Arab Republic had disintegrated six years earlier) got wind of an alleged Israeli military build-up on the Syrian frontier. They called on Egypt for help and Nasser felt obliged to respond. Although a large proportion of the Egyptian Armed Forces were mired in the civil war between republicans and royalists in the Yemen, Nasser reoccupied Sinai and demanded the withdrawal of the United Nations force. The U.N. Secretary-General complied – constitutionally the force could only remain in being with the agreement of the parties to the dispute – and Nasser closed the Straits of Tiran at the southern end of the north-eastern fork of the Red Sea. Bahraini friends were dining with us when this news came through and I remember saying to them that this meant war: the Israelis would never allow their only southern point of access to the outside world to be blocked. A few weeks of frantic international diplomacy ensued and the temperatures rose in Bahrain as the bombast from Cairo Radio scaled hitherto unprecedented heights. On the 6th of June we awoke to the news that the war had started.

A few hours later I heard the 'Big Lie' being spread by Arab radio stations. This story was that British and American aircraft had participated in the Israeli surprise attack on Egyptian Air Force bases at dawn on 6th June. This attack had in fact won the war in an hour or so, the Egyptian ground forces in Sinai being left without air cover. In no time demonstrators were swirling and chanting outside the gates of the Agency. The next four or five days were confused and hectic. The flames of excitement burnt high in Bahrain and the Agency was surrounded by shouting crowds from early morning until late at night. In spite of the 'Big Lie' they were not actively hostile, although I would not have described their attitude as friendly. I remember for example that, in the middle of the war, a group of American and British executives called at my office to discuss the aluminium smelter project. They arrived early, before the demonstrators: an hour later we were hemmed in. The Head of the Bahrain Development Bureau telephoned and asked me to bring the visitors to his office in the Government Secretariat Building, a walk of about a hundred yards across an open space now thronged with demonstrators. I confess that I felt a little anxious; what would we do if, on our opening the gate to the Agency courtyard, the demonstrators either poured in or blocked our exit? We walked out – those accompanying me were, as I recall, on their first visit to the Middle East – and I gestured to the crowd pressing against the gate to open a path and let us through. They fell back. We walked a little self-consciously forward through the throng, many of whom knew me by sight, and reached the Secretariat unharmed. I heard afterwards that the delegation had been greatly impressed by the underlying stability of Bahrain at a time when Arab emotion was at such a height, and that this incident had strongly influenced them in favour of going ahead with the project.

The situation was confused by the fact that totally contradictory accounts from the battlefield were pouring in simultaneously. While the B.B.C. and the Western press, as well of course as my confidential telegrams, were reporting an unqualified disaster to Arab arms, Cairo Radio and Damascus Radio were thundering away about brilliant Arab victories, spouting blood-curdling threats against the Israeli leadership and giving the overall impression that the fall of Tel Aviv was imminent. I used to listen regularly to Cairo Radio and, although I had no doubt in my mind of where the truth lay, the clamour of lies was so deafening that even I used occasionally to wonder if the Arabs were really doing as badly as my information suggested. How could the unfortunate Bahraini people be expected to distil the truth out of this farrago of rhetoric? It became increasingly clear to me that they were in for a nasty shock and that disillusionment might breed an ugly temper. The time came when even Cairo and Damascus were forced to admit that it was all over. In less than a week the Israelis had seized Sinai up to the Suez Canal, the Gaza Strip, the West Bank including Jerusalem, and the Syrian Golan Heights. The Egyptian, Jordanian and Syrian armed forces had been smashed. The truth could no longer be concealed: the Arabs had been beaten.

As ecstasy plunged to despair, the mood of the demonstrators outside the Agency soured and freedom of movement for myself, my family and my staff became more difficult. One evening – it must have been the 12th or 13th of June – I was told that we were in for an unpleasant surprise. Elements in the crowd were making arrangements to provide themselves with arms. The following morning they planned to stir up the majority, attack the Agency and burn it down. There were other buildings in the town which were similarly marked down for the torch.

My staff and I conferred and agreed on our dispositions. I refused the offer of troops from the British base to protect the Agency. I believed that their arrival would provoke the crowd and that, if an attack developed and they were forced to open fire, the long-term political effect of British troops having shot Bahrainis would be disastrous, to put it mildly. By the same token I disarmed the Agency guard of about a dozen N.C.O.s and men from the Bahrain State Police and deployed them inside the building, out of sight. So far as I was concerned, no shots would be fired from a Diplomatic Mission. We then locked all our interior doors (and subsequently lost most of the keys) in order to impede the progress of anyone breaking in. Our tactics were for the male staff and the policemen to confront the crowd in the lobby and first to try to prevent an invasion by argument, and then, if that failed, to hold the staircase if we could. If the assault was pressed with determination, our plan was to retreat up the stairs and thence, by an outside staircase, into the garden where the female staff plus my wife, nanny and baby would be waiting. The rioters could then do their worst with the building. Given the basically good-natured character of the islanders, I do not think that it occurred to any of us that we would be in physical danger.

By this time the crowd had gathered in even larger numbers than usual and I could see rifles being waved about. Their mood had changed for the worse. We waited. After half an hour or so of chanting and exhortation, it looked as though an attack was imminent. The telephone rang. It was Shaikh Isa, calling to ask how things were going. I explained our predicament and our plans, emphasising that there was no danger to life and limb, only to our property. The Ruler did not seem disposed to acquiesce in damage being done to the property of foreigners living in his territory. I stressed that I was asking for nothing and we resumed waiting. About twenty minutes later I saw a large black car, the Ruler's, drive slowly into the middle of the by now highly excited crowd. Shaikh Isa was alone except for his driver: there was no escort car. He got out and stood on the bonnet. I was just out of earshot but he was clearly delivering a powerful harangue. He re-entered the car which drove off in the direction of the town at a walking pace. The large crowd followed quietly: ten minutes later the open space in front of the Agency was empty: we relaxed and returned to our normal work after an intensive search had revealed the majority of the keys to our doors! It had been a stimulating morning with a truly remarkable climax. I shall never forget it.

Over the next few days we took stock. In spite of the tempest of emotion which had gripped the island, there had been only one minor clash – between a small group of Arab and Persian youths. A few windows of houses and cars belonging to British military personnel had been broken. The cost of this damage ran to less than five hundred pounds which Shaikh Isa paid within minutes of my presenting him with the bill. Bahrain had given an astonishing demonstration of restraint and stability under maximum stress.

For weeks, indeed for months, the population was seized by the gloom of disillusionment and the reaction following high tension. But the external pressures on the loyalties of the people disappeared. The radical Arab governments in Cairo and Damascus realised that they needed the status quo in the oil-bearing Arab states in order to ensure the free flow of oil, and the money deriving from it, to rebuild after the crushing defeat. Within days of the end of hostilities, the Cairo radio station, Voice of the Arab Gulf, was closed down: the Voice of the Arabs moderated its previous raptures, and support for dissident groups ceased. Bahrain calmed down and even the transfer to the island of a substantial British military headquarters with ancillary units, following our withdrawal from Aden, passed virtually unnoticed and entirely unopposed. We began to live in a different world.

However, for us, the British diplomats, and for the government of Bahrain, the year was not to end without further alarms. By the autumn, following a sterling crisis in London, stories were beginning to circulate of an imminent British withdrawal from 'East of Suez', including the Gulf. Agitation mounted amongst the Rulers. It was not that they were congenitally opposed to assuming responsibility for the conduct of their foreign policy or for their own defence. But, with their free and aristocratic tribal backgrounds, they had no 'colonial' chips on their shoulders regarding their relationship with Britain. Their present anxiety arose from a number of causes. Apart from Oman, there were no indigenous defence forces in the area, only police and the Trucial Oman Scouts commanded by the Political Resident. Also the Gulf was a rich prey for external predators. Iran claimed Bahrain and Saudi Arabia had claims against parts of Oman and Abu Dhabi. Most of the states had border disputes with each other. With these problems unsolved, the nine states considered themselves in no condition to confront the heavy seas of full independence.

In November, the newly appointed Minister of State at the Foreign and Commonwealth Office, Mr Goronwy Roberts, toured the Gulf and spoke to all the Rulers. He also made public statements in Bahrain to the B.B.C. Arabic Service and to the Editor of the only Arabic-language newspaper, *Al Adhwa'a*. His message was the same in all cases. Britain had no intention of withdrawing from the Gulf. Britain would stay in the Gulf as long as its presence was necessary to maintain peace and security in the area and thus to ensure economic and social development.

The Gulf relaxed and we were able to enjoy our Christmas and New Year celebrations in a more tranquil frame of mind than had seemed possible at any time during what had been a seismic year.

We were not left in peace for long. In January 1968 we were told that Mr Goronwy Roberts would be paying us another visit. The burden of his second message to the Rulers was not imparted to me until immediately before his arrival, but I picked up enough gossip from British travellers passing through Bahrain to realise that we were in for an unpleasant surprise. I was not at liberty to speculate with the Ruler and his government about Mr Roberts's reasons for coming to see us again after an interval of only two months. But Shaikh Isa was such a close friend that I could not bring myself flatly to refuse to answer his questions. I confined myself to saying that we could be pretty sure that Mr Roberts was not travelling all the way to the Gulf to wish the Rulers a Happy New Year! Since his message on the previous occasion had been unexpectedly reassuring, Shaikh Isa would be wise to prepare his mind to hear something unwelcome.

Mr Roberts arrived and we went over his brief together. As I had anticipated the government had decided, principally as it appeared for financial reasons, to announce that Britain would terminate its military presence in the Gulf (and with it the protective treaties with the Gulf states) at the end of 1971. The Minister of State was stopping in Bahrain for a few hours only and we discussed his mission in my car en route for the Ruler's Palace. I made no bones about the fact that what he had to say would come as a violent shock to Shaikh Isa. All Bahrain had been expecting this blow to fall when the Minister paid his November visit. The fact that, on that occasion, he had reassured the Rulers had led to a wave of relief which would make his present announcement all the more inexplicable and difficult to accept. He need not expect Shaikh Isa to blow up in his face – that would be contrary to Arab tradition with a guest – but he should not imagine that this would mean that the impact would be any the less.

We arrived at the Palace and stopped the car for a few minutes in the road outside in order to finish our discussion. We could see the Guard of Honour drawn up with the Ruler and his brother, Shaikh Khalifah, standing by the door to the private Majlis. We entered and sat down to the meeting. Mr Roberts told the shaikhs that, on his last visit, he had been unable to give them a time limit to the British military presence in the Gulf. He was now able to do so: we would be terminating our military presence at the end of 1971. The two shaikhs received this bombshell with impassive courtesy and all the rituals demanded by good manners were gone through. We were not there for more than half an hour. As we drove off, Mr Roberts showed signs of relief and suggested to me that the encounter had not gone too badly. I repeated my warning that he should not judge by appearances.

After I had seen Mr Roberts off at the airport I was summoned to the Palace where I was exposed to a full and detailed exposition of the Ruler's reaction to what he had been told by the Minister of State. I returned to the Agency and reported this second conversation to London. The deed was done and that was that. But I was deeply troubled about my personal position and slept little that night. On Mr Roberts's first visit in November, the whole island had expected that his purpose was to announce a date for British military withdrawal and the termination of the treaties. I had made this clear to the Minister and had received unequivocal confirmation that we were all wrong. Had it been otherwise, although I would not have agreed with the decision, I would have faithfully represented the new policy. Between November and January I had frequently reassured the Bahrain government that the decision to stay was final and that they should put all other thoughts out of their minds. How could I now confront this volte-face and retain my own honour? I realised that, if I were to resign, this act would change nothing and would not create even a ripple on the surface of events. But these were not reasons for failing to do the right thing. As dawn broke I had come close to deciding that I must go. After breakfast I went down to my office to start the day's work, although my mind was in no condition to concentrate on my daily routine of business. I had not been long at my desk when an emissary from the Palace brought me an oral message from the Ruler. It was short and pertinent. 'Tony, we know what you are thinking: you are not to resign.' As the morning wore on, I received virtually identical telephone calls from close friends in the Bahrain government. I was deeply moved, not simply by this flattering display of confidence, but by the fact that these messages demonstrated how well we had come to know each other, and that my friends should have shown such sympathetic consideration for my feelings at such a time. I decided to stay on and to do the best I could in the new set of circumstances.

When they had recovered from the shock, the Ruling Family and the government set about tackling the future with realism. In late 1967, in anticipation of this development, Shaikh Isa had decided to create a small, indigenous Defence Force. These plans were now accelerated. Furthermore the pressure of events created a new dynamic towards union in all the Gulf states: it was announced in February 1968 that agreement had been reached in Abu Dhabi to establish a Union of Arab Emirates, comprising Bahrain, Qatar and the seven Trucial States. The British decision had in fact stimulated a drive towards unity which all our previous efforts had failed to create.

This announcement sparked off a public debate in Bahrain and a wave of intergovernmental activity which was still flowing when I left the island a year later. Opinions were divided. The younger, educated generation were generally enthusiastic about the prospect of a union of the Nine. Others, including myself, believed that, although a union of the seven small states on the coast was essential, Bahrain was different. Its population was larger, it was geographically distant from the Seven, and its nature and history were distinct from those of the smaller shaikhdoms. Moreover, Bahrain was just large enough to sustain full independence on its own. My private feeling was that a union of the Nine would not work and that Bahrain would be best advised to go it alone. The need for fresh economic development projects became more pressing. The British military presence was creating a disproportionate amount of economic activity as well as injecting large sums of money into the islands. Rents, local purchases, the employment of Bahraini staff in the various installations, the construction industry, transport, etc., had become important ingredients in local prosperity. Other sources had to be found to fill what would be a major gap and it was fortunate that the projected aluminium smelter and graving dock were now at an advanced planning stage.

But the Iranian claim loomed darkly over both political and economic development. The Shah of Iran made it clear that Iran would have nothing to do with a union which included Bahrain, thus sowing seeds of doubt and hesitation amongst the other Rulers. Equally important, the claim was having a stultifying effect on Bahrain's economy. The island, with its sophisticated facilities, advanced communications and agreeable atmosphere, was the ideal place for banks and other businesses to establish themselves in order to conduct operations throughout the Gulf area and southern Iran. But the Iranian refusal to do business with or to communicate with Bahrain virtually precluded foreign enterprises from taking this step.

The claim was also a source of political neurosis against the prospect of the removal of British protection: to the Bahrainis it was not merely a diplomatic dispute, it was reality. I remember an occasion in 1968 which illustrates this well. I was driving on Muharraq Island when I suddenly found the road choked by a shouting mob of people from the town, carrying sticks and stones and running towards the airport. I stopped one of them and asked him what was happening. 'The Persians, the Persians, they have landed,' he shouted. For a moment I could not imagine what on earth had started this panic. I then saw a civil aircraft on the apron with a large tail fin emblazoned with a lion (British Caledonian). The lion is (or was) the national symbol of Iran. The good citizens of Muharraq, spotting this aircraft, had assumed that an Iranian airborne force had landed, and were rushing to the scene to repel the invaders!

What was the Bahrain government to do, with unprotected independence less than four years away and the Shah implacable? Rely on Saudi Arabia and the Arab League as a whole to maintain Bahrain's integrity? Defend herself against Iran? Neither expedient seemed to offer a secure future and all attempts at a negotiated settlement over more than a century had failed. My personal view was that, in the absence of a settlement, the Bahrain government would have no choice. They would have to grasp the nettle and apply for membership of the United Nations while British troops were still in situ. Bahrain would have full Arab support which would eliminate the risk of a Soviet veto in the

Security Council. I could not envisage any of the other Permanent Members – Britain, France, the United States or (Nationalist) China – blocking a Bahraini application and I had no doubt that the General Assembly would vote overwhelmingly in favour of Bahrain's admission: Iran had few friends. The Iranians would scream and shout and refuse to recognise the new member. The economic obstacles would remain but I doubted whether Iran would dare actually to invade and annex a full member of the international community: the penalties, particularly from the Great Powers, would be too high. I did not delude myself that this would be a satisfactory outcome but I could see no alternative. One thing was certain. Bahrain was an Arab country and would not willingly allow herself to be incorporated as the 14th province of Iran.

Fortunately, a month or so before I left Bahrain, the Shah performed an act of statesmanship which at last opened the way to a mutually satisfactory solution. While on a State visit to India in, I think, December 1968 the Shah stated publicly (I forget his exact words) that, although he had no doubt that Bahrain was part of Iran, the population might have changed over the years: he would therefore be prepared to accept their verdict on their future provided that their views could be freely expressed and independently verified. This statement, with its clear implication of acceptance of Bahraini self-determination, changed the whole picture.

Shortly before this dramatic statement was made, I had been told by London that I would be transferred in the New Year to the United Kingdom Mission to the United Nations in New York, thus beginning an association with the U.N. which was to last until my retirement many years later. The prospect was exciting and the change could not have been more marked, from the cosy intimacy of bilateral diplomacy in a small island in the Gulf to the global centre of multilateral diplomacy in one of the greatest cities in the world. My wife's and my feelings were mixed. We had fallen in love with Bahrain. We had a host of intimate friends among the Al Khalifah family, Bahraini officials, merchants and others in the foreign community. Our uncomplicated life with our small daughter, now three years old, and our older children who visited us for holidays, suited us well. We felt that the extent to which we had become part of the Bahraini scene was greater than had been the case in any of the other countries in which we had served. Professionally my life had been full of interest from the outset, and my peculiar position as Political Agent had secured for me a closeness of contact with all aspects of Bahraini life denied to diplomats in more conventional circumstances. And, in my varied observation of Arab politics, I had discovered a system which, in the circumstances of a small and tightly knit community, worked. There might be dissent and dissatisfaction over certain issues, but the basic problem of legitimacy which had haunted the monarchy in Iraq and for which the revolutionaries in Cairo had struggled so hard with their political experimentation, was absent. The mechanisms of democratic representation might be lacking but the people could express their views to the political arm of government (the Ruler in open council) with a reasonable certainty that the Ruler would incorporate them into an eventual consensus, while the functional arm (the modern administration) operated as well if not better than any other which I had encountered.

Nor was it a static society. I had seen many changes. The older generation of shaikhs, the Ruler's uncles and great-uncles, had gradually withdrawn from active participation in public affairs and were being replaced by a younger generation, many of them technically well qualified for the posts they assumed. More young, educated Bahrainis of non-shaikhly origin were entering the administration, which was expanding to meet the demands of a more complex world. The economy was beginning to pick up. By the time of my departure, the Agency, against which the tide had lapped on my arrival, was nearly a mile inland with large buildings, including a governmental centre, under construction on reclaimed land. Isa Town, which I had passed as a building site on my first call on the Ruler, was flourishing with some thousands of inhabitants. A Technical College, a timely British initiative, was under construction to serve the higher technical educational needs of all the states of the southern Gulf. The domestic malaise which I had sensed in 1965 had evaporated and Bahrain was facing the future with growing confidence.

Our farewells were protracted and emotional: the kindness of our friends made parting even more difficult. The day before we left, my wife and I lunched alone with Shaikh Isa in his small villa on his private beach for the last time. We talked about the past, the experiences through which we had lived together, and the future. When it came to saying goodbye I was very moved. The next morning we were gone.

Postscript. I arrived in New York to find my Bahraini connexion unbroken. It had been decided to invoke the good offices of the Secretary-General of the United Nations, U Thant, to follow up the Shah's Delhi statement. Because of my Bahraini past, my boss, Lord Caradon, delegated the detailed negotiating to me. For over a year I had a series of meetings with Dr Ralph Bunche, the Under-Secretary-General responsible for Security questions, and with the Iranian delegation. The objective was, with the agreement of the governments of Iran, Bahrain and Britain, to devise a mechanism by which the views of the people of Bahrain could be tested and the results submitted for the approval of the U.N. Security Council. It was a long and difficult business. Dr Bunche was mortally ill and nearly blind, but mentally as alert as ever. In spite of his infirmity his devotion was total: I remember his flying to and from Europe in the bitter winter of 1969–70 to attend personally to some aspect of the negotiations and calling me to his office on his return: it was Christmas Eve and the thermometer was below zero. Dr Bunche was on his last legs and I had to read the documents aloud to him. In the end the stage was set and, in early 1970, Dr Winspeare Guiccardi, an Italian official of the U.N. Secretariat, with terms of reference agreed by all parties, visited Bahrain to ascertain the wishes of the people. He spoke to individuals, to community leaders, to representatives of clubs and associations, to village headmen and many others. In April he submitted his report to the Secretary-General who transmitted it to the Security Council. His recommendation was clear: Bahraini opinion was overwhelmingly resolved that Bahrain should be an independent Arab state. The Security Council met in open session and adopted a resolution to that effect unanimously. The Iranian delegation participated in the proceedings, although not members of the Council, and co-sponsored the resolution with Britain. Behind the horseshoe of the Council, in the seats reserved for visiting delegates, sat a mission from Bahrain led by Shaikh Mohammed bin Mubarak, Foreign Minister designate, who had met me on my first arrival at Muharraq Airport five years before. The ancient claim was at last laid to rest and a major road-block across the path of Bahrain's future was removed. It was May 1970. 'In my end is my beginning.'

Fifteen years later

It is the 30th of November 1984 and the aircraft in which my wife and I are travelling is coming in to land at Muharraq Airport. In my time the runway was too short to enable an aircraft of this size to land: now, in the darkness, it stretches for miles. We enter the glittering and palatial terminal building which has replaced the small cluster of low buildings of fifteen years ago. We drive into Manama along a wide, dual carriageway, flanked by rows of neat villas. Can this be where the labyrinth of small streets of Muharraq used to be? And where is the causeway? At last I see the water briefly on both sides of the road: land reclamation has crept forward, almost joining the two islands. The old Agency seems to have disappeared. Instead of passing it we swing right along a broad corniche and find ourselves among tall, modern buildings. The car draws up at the door of the Bahrain Sheraton. We are shown into a luxurious suite. It is two o'clock in the morning, not long to wait until we can see our surroundings by daylight.

In the morning we call on the Amir (Shaikh Isa is no longer known as the Ruler), his brother the Prime Minister and his cousin, the Foreign Minister, at the new Government Centre. Our close friend Yousuf Shirawi, now Minister of Industry and Development, then shows us the island. The British Embassy (the old Agency), once the largest and most imposing building on the seafront, is lost amongst the high buildings: Sheraton, Regency, Inter-Continental, Gulf International Bank, Bank of America – the roll of honour of a thriving commercial centre. We drive west through extensive suburbs and country villages trans-formed by newly built houses. We reach a project which, in my time, was talked about only as a distant, theoretical possibility – a combination of causeway and bridges linking Bahrain to the mainland of Saudi Arabia. Our guide, with characteristic Bahraini informality, is driving his own car with no escort. After explaining to a bewildered Dutch en-gineer that he is the Minister responsible for the project, Yousuf drives us on to the causeway, which stretches almost the full distance of about fifteen miles to the opposite shore. We pass small islands which we had known from our boat-ing expeditions of long ago, the prison island of Jida, the island belonging to the Amir's youngest brother, the island of Umm el Nassan, home of a herd of gazelle imported from India by the Amir's grandfather. The causeway is a remarkable feat of civil engineering which reflects great cre-dit on the Dutch contractors. If I revisit Bahrain in a year's time it will be complete and full of cars and lorries going in both directions – Bahrain's channel tunnel; an island no longer. Will this physical link with the mainland modify in the long term the fundamentally insular character of the people of Bahrain, the only substantially inhabited island in the Arab world? It is this insularity which has given Bahrain a stronger sense of nationhood than can be found almost anywhere in the region, except in Egypt and Turkey. Will the specifically Bahraini nature of the people survive once the mainland is accessible by a ten-minute car drive? Many Bahrainis are asking themselves these and related questions. Will the causeway lead to an exodus of the Bahraini labour force to make money in the new industrial complexes of eastern Saudi Arabia? Will tariff adjustment be necessary to avoid the possibility that Bahrainis will do their daily shop-ping across the water, thus damaging local markets? Will the Wahhabi religious hierarchy object to their people being exposed to Bahrain's more relaxed atmosphere and bring pressure on the government to adopt their puritanical practices? If so, what effect will this have on international commerce and finance in the island? Militarily, will the causeway present a tempting target or provide easy access for troops to rush to Bahrain's assistance in time of need? Only time will supply the answers.

Our guided tour continues down wide roads where before there were not even desert tracks, past new towns - Isa Town now complete and Hamad Town (named after the Crown Prince) shortly to provide cheap housing for thousands more families - private villas of the well-to-do, industrial and trading estates, the aluminium smelter boiling in the distance, the graving dock far out in the bay.

I am taken to the Rifa'a Palace, thinking of my first drive to call on the Ruler nearly twenty years previously. Now the road through the suburbs of Manama is unrecognisable and the outskirts join with Isa Town, which stretches almost to Rifa'a: the open country has virtually disappeared. But when I reach the palace, I find that little has changed. There is still only a small guard from the Bahrain State Police. The salukis and the falcons have gone and there are no familiar faces among the retainers. But here again is the Amir, waiting to greet me as of old: we walk together into the private Majlis - he has just finished the morning open session - and sit side by side at the end of the room as we had done so many times before. We talk, mainly of bygone, more difficult times before Bahrain achieved the prosperity of which I have already seen so much evidence.

In the next couple of days my wife and I begin to form impressions. Much has changed. Bahrain is no longer by any definition an 'oil shaikhdom': revenue from indigenous oil is negligible although a fair amount of Saudi oil is still being refined and the products exported. With the obstacle of the Iranian claim removed, with the accretion of wealth in the region following the oil boom of the 1970s, with its more easy-going environment compared to the austerities of the mainland, and with the collapse of Beirut, the old business capital of the Middle East, Bahrain has reverted to the role it has played in the Gulf since Babylonian days, that of an international centre for commerce, finance and communications. Many foreign firms have chosen Bahrain as their headquarters for regional operations, offshore banking and insurance companies have poured in, entrepôt trade has flourished and enough local industry has been established to provide significant employment. The government has become (with Saudi financial assistance) a provider – of health services, of education, of communications, of public works. Under the umbrella of this general welfare, the private sector has energised the day-to-day economy. Our fears of the 1960s have evaporated. The population, including foreigners, has nearly doubled to about 400,000. But there is no Bahraini unemployment – at least not so far as we could judge in a very short visit. On the contrary there are more foreigners than ever, due to a shortage of labour and the exponential expansion of the economy. The British community is close to 7000, more than the combined total of British military and civilians in the days of British protection. Indians, Pakistanis, Filipinos, Thais, Sri Lankans, Bangladeshis work on building sites, in hotels, offices and shops. Manama, which was a sleepy, rustic Arab town, is now a bustling cosmopolitan place with twentieth-century facilities familiar to travellers of the world from Los Angeles to Singapore.

And yet, under this gleaming surface, there is much that has remained the same. The bazaar area of Manama is richer but still recognisable with its mosques and courtyards opening from narrow streets. The wealthy merchant families are much more so but their way of life is the same. There is no question, as was the case in the Shah's Iran, of wealth bringing with it personal ostentation – the luxurious suites of offices in the penthouses of tower buildings, the boss guarded by dazzling European/American-style secretaries. We call by chance in the bazaar on a friend of ours, the son of one of the leading families in the island. There he is, as his father used to be, in his small, hot office in the same old building, the ante-room crowded with a flow of people coming and going with no appointments or formalities. 'May I see Sayed Ali?' I ask. 'He is a friend of mine.' 'You want to see Sayed Hussein, you mean,' replies the old

143

toothless doorkeeper, 'you are more his age.' 'No, I mean Sayed Ali; could you please telephone him?' 'Telephone, telephone: no need for that. Just walk in. You'll find him there.' After the modernities of the Bahrain Sheraton, I find this exchange consoling.

The nature of the government too has not changed. The functional side, the structure of Ministries and Departments, has expanded and can no longer be accommodated in one building as in the past. The machine has of necessity become more systematised, more bureaucratic. But the old informality remains close to the surface. The political side has altered even less. A brief experiment in the 1970s with an elected parliament was abandoned after a year or two without, as it appears, any hostile reaction from the people, and even the municipal elections which used to take place in my time have died of inanition and lack of public interest. Shaikh Isa still sits in his open council, as does the Prime Minister, and the people at all levels can still maintain their direct access to their rulers: they in turn can by this process of two-way communication gauge the level and quality of public reaction to government policies and act accordingly. In a nutshell the dual system of traditional rule and modern administration has survived full independence, membership of the international community, and the economic and social changes which prosperity has brought in its wake. Bahrain is a remarkable phenomenon, a sophisticated, literate, urban society, a cosmopolitan financial centre, still ruled by the same Family and in the same style as it was in the eighteenth century. Would a change to a more modern, representational system, based on Western models, have produced better results, a more stable society, even more genuine participation by the people in the decision-making process? I wonder.

It is an important part of the job of a diplomat to predict the future. It is also one of the most difficult tasks. The view down the telescope focused on the future is too often clouded and distorted by knowledge of the present and the past. Absorbed in the minutiae of the present, the observer tends to see the past as a continuum which is likely to extend along its metalled rails into the future. In analysing the past, it is easy to overlook the key role played by chance in the passage of events. Take the case of Bahrain. When I left the country in 1969 our minds and those of the Bahraini leaders were filled with a catalogue of anxieties. Would the economy survive the withdrawal of the British military presence without serious unemployment creating political turbulence? What would happen about the Iranian claim after the termination of British protection? Would the British military withdrawal be accompanied by terrorism as happened in Aden? Would there be a resurgence of pan-Arab nationalism directed from Cairo, which would prove too potent a force for the traditional regimes in the Arabian peninsula?

Now, fifteen years later, these preoccupations have an archaic flavour. The Iranian claim has been settled peacefully, and the economy is booming as it has never boomed before. The anticipated ghost towns of empty houses and barracks abandoned by the retreating British never materialised. We terminated our protective relationship peacefully, in friendship and with dignity – a vivid contrast to the disorderly scramble out of Aden. Bahrain is now a respected member of the Arab League, on excellent terms with all Arab states except for one or two unimportant eccentrics. The days of the trumpeting of the Voice of the Arabs and the Voice of the Gulf seem like a page out of prehistory.

Of course the country is not without a fresh set of anxieties, none of which could have been anticipated by the observers of the 1960s (by the time this book is published the pattern may well have changed again). Bahrain's eastern neighbour, Iran, is now ruled by Ayatollah Khomeini and the activists amongst the large Bahraini Shia community are susceptible to his stern, evangelical message. There have been plots and assassination attempts, all so far discovered in time. But the danger remains. Furthermore Iran and Iraq have now been at war for more than four years and the fear is always present that the reciprocal attacks on shipping and shore installations may spread to the islands. Interestingly, this threat of war has stimulated a degree of co-operation between the Gulf states and Saudi Arabia which could not have been imagined in the old days: the possibility of a joint military force is under discussion and Bahrain may have to contribute a contingent from its small but, to outward appearances, well-trained Defence Force. How times have changed.

Our short visit is over and it is time to say goodbye again. We have said our farewells to the Amir after an enchanting day on his yacht, to Yousuf Shirawi who has given up so much of his busy time to show us the differences between Bahrain 1984 and Bahrain 1969. Appropriately we lunch, an hour or two before our aircraft takes off for Kuwait, with the Foreign Minister, Shaikh Mohammed bin Mubarak, and another old friend, the former Bahraini Ambassador to London. Parting is hard, as it was fifteen years before, and, as the reader will by this time have surmised, a large part of our hearts remains behind.

Epilogue

For well over a hundred and fifty years, British power and influence relentlessly impregnated the Eastern Arab world. The process was as gradual as the spread of ink on blotting paper. First, in the early nineteenth century, the stain crept along the shore of the Arabian peninsula from the Persian Gulf to the Red Sea. By the end of the century it had extended and sunk deep into Egypt and the Sudan. By the 1920s it had reached Palestine, Transjordan and Iraq. By 1945 Britain appeared supreme and virtually unchallenged by outside and regional powers from Libya to the borders of Afghanistan. Now forty years later, the tide has receded, leaving Britain as no more than one of many states with major interests in the region, of less importance to the Arabs than the United States, the Soviet Union and, improbably, France, although history and folk memory will for many years accord to 'the British' a special place in Arab minds.

The flowing tide carried with it a growing multitude of British people – traders, soldiers, officials, administrators, engineers, teachers, travellers, diplomats, specialists of all kinds. As the preceding chapters have revealed, I was one of them, arriving as a young soldier at the high-water mark of the highest spring tide, leaving about thirty years later as a middle-aged diplomat, one of the last relics beached by the withdrawal of the water, which had by then receded from all the land it had once covered.

Now, in my retirement, I reflect on the question: what have we given, what legacy remains and will remain in the future, bequeathed to the Arabs by Britain over this crucial period in their and our history, dating effectively from the

Napoleonic invasion of Egypt in 1798 to the termination of the British protective treaties with the Arab states of the Persian Gulf in 1971?

Ask any Arab this question and he would be likely to reply that Britain's most enduring and terrible legacy to the Middle East has been the problem of Palestine. He would say that this is a burden which Britain neither can nor should try to evade. 'You the British', he would say, 'were the people who made promises to the Arabs in 1915 in order to rouse them to revolt against the Turks. You the British did the bulk of the fighting which, by 1918, had driven the Turks out of most of what is now Syria, Lebanon, Iraq, Jordan and the Arabian peninsula. But you the British also issued the Balfour Declaration in 1917, stating that His Majesty's Government "views with favour the establishment in Palestine of a national home for the Jewish people and will use their best endeavours to facilitate this object". This compromised, to say the least, the undertakings already made to the Arabs. You the British then arrogated to yourselves and had confirmed by the League of Nations a Mandate over Palestine comprising the terms of the Balfour Declaration including the provision: "It being clearly understood that nothing shall be done to prejudice the civil and religious rights of other non-Jewish communities in Palestine" (a curious way to describe 90 per cent of the population at the time the Declaration was issued). You the British, during the twenty-five years of your Mandate failed for all your efforts – and you made many in good faith – to implement this latter provision. In 1948 you abandoned the Mandate to a United Nations sponsored solution – partition – in which you did not believe. You left it to war to decide. Now half the Arab population of Palestine are refugees and the other half are living under Israeli occupation: the Arabs and the Israelis have fought five or six major wars with each other: the casualties run into hundreds of thousands: peace is as far away as ever: the poison of Palestine has infected the whole region, it has drawn the super-powers into the Middle East and poses perhaps the most serious threat to world peace outside the Central European confrontation. You now have no power and, without power, responsibilities cannot be discharged. But we will never let you forget that this is your main bequest to us.'

I do not think that this is an exaggerated statement of the Arab case against Britain. And it is not easy to refute. Admittedly, in 1917, Britain had its back to the wall. We needed Jewish support from America. We needed to counter the blandishments of the Central Powers to the Jews of Europe. We needed to mobilise the support of the Jewish elements in revolutionary Russia, still in the war against Germany. For biblical and romantic reasons, there was a strong pro-Jewish sentiment amongst many British political leaders. But did we have the right, even in those imperialistic days, to pre-empt on behalf of a third party a territory to which we had no claim, without regard to the wishes of the people of that land? Was it even expedient to adopt a commitment which, to anyone with any knowledge of the region, contained a contradiction certain to make its implementation in full an impossibility? One side or the other was bound to suffer.

I would certainly not deny the rights of the Jews, after centuries of persecution, degradation and massacre at the hands of Europeans, to a national home in which they can live in peace, not as second-class citizens. But should we have enforced that right at the expense of a people, the Arabs, who did not share the guilt of Europe towards Jewish communities? Certainly the Jews now have their national home. But, nearly seventy years after the Balfour Declaration was proclaimed, the Jewish state still has to live as a garrison surrounded by hostile nations, permanently under arms and severed from its natural trading and cultural partners.

And I have seen with my own eyes, ever since I left Palestine in 1948, how this unsolved problem has infected the whole region. Time was when it was possible to have conversations with Arabs on subjects other than Palestine. Now this is no longer the case, from the shores of the Persian Gulf to the Sudan and beyond. Palestine has become the cardinal point of reference for the domestic politics of Arab states, for the relationship between member states of the Arab League, for the conduct of Arab diplomacy with the outside world. Palestine has turned the region into an armed camp. The embryonic military forces of the regional states in the late 1940s have been transformed into massive arsenals. Any one of five or six states in the region probably possesses more battle tanks and front-line combat aircraft than any NATO or Warsaw Pact power with the exception of the United States and the Soviet Union. It was the perceived need for arms in connexion with this dispute which enabled the Soviet Union to penetrate the Arab world in 1955, thus triggering off an unprecedented East/West competition of political and military support for regional states, not to speak of Israel's development of a nuclear capability. For nearly forty years Palestine has dominated the agenda of the United Nations. The Middle East has been the principal area to which United Nations peace-keeping forces have had to be despatched. More resolutions have been laid before the Security Council on the Middle East than on any other area of international concern. I could extend the list of consequences further to include, for example, the oil price rise of 1973 which fundamentally changed the economy of the world, the collapse of the Lebanon as a viable state from 1975 onwards, and much more. Palestine has, in a nutshell, become one of the most pervasive and dramatic of global problems since the end of the Second World War. Strange to think that it all began with a short, one-sentence letter from the British Foreign Secretary to Lord Rothschild in November 1917.

Is there anything effective which Britain can do now to redeem the pledge which we failed to meet on behalf of 'other non-Jewish communities in Palestine', that is to say, is there anything we can do either to promote a peaceful settlement of the dispute in which all parties would acquiesce, or, failing that, to relieve the misery of the Palestinian Arabs in the refugee camps or living under Israeli occupation? Precious little, I fear, now that we are shorn of the power to move events. All we can do diplomatically, bilaterally or preferably as part of a consensus of the European Community, is to use our residual influence with all concerned – to persuade the Israelis that genuine peace is of greater value than the retention of the Arab territory occupied in 1967 plus continued existence as a garrison state, to persuade the Arabs that the terms of Security Council Resolution 242 of 1967 (essentially a peace treaty which recognises the state of Israel behind secure boundaries approximating to the Armistice Lines of 1967) combined with an act of self-determination for the Palestinians in the remainder of what used to be Mandatory Palestine (the West Bank and Gaza) are preferable to a combination of mutual hostility and inter-Arab divisions, to persuade the United States to exert itself without relaxation of effort to achieve the above objectives, rather than galvanising itself into action only when crisis situations demand it and turning its back when immediate danger recedes. Ultimately there can be no doubt that the dispute must be settled between the parties themselves. But the rift between them runs so deep that outside influence will be required to bring them together, perhaps to set out the guidelines for a solution – as the United Nations has already done – and then to ensure that both sides are prepared to show the flexibility necessary to ensure progress. Whether or not such negotiations take place under United Nations auspices, the main burden will rest on the United States. Other powers, such as Britain and France or the European Community as a whole, can hope to influence the Arabs in the direction of moderation, but only the Americans can hope to influence Israel, and it is Israel which must give up territory if there is to be peace.

In the mean time, and the mean time is likely to be very long judging by the history of the dispute, Britain should be prepared to do a great deal more by way of financial aid and economic development for the Palestinians in the occupied territories. It is a source of shame that the former Mandatory Power, which must bear heavy responsibility for the plight of the Palestinians, is currently producing less in aid to the occupied territories than the British voluntary agencies. So far as I know, the sum in question is around £100,000 a year, a derisory amount. Surely we should be doing a great deal more than this, in spite of the difficulties involved in ensuring that aid reaches the people in need in circumstances of foreign military occupation, considering that the overall British overseas aid budget must be well in excess of £1000 million. I am not suggesting that even ten or one hundred times our present contribution would fundamentally alter the economic and social condition of the occupied territories. But a respectable aid programme consonant both with our historical responsibility and our present financial position, would not only do some practical good: it would also do something for the morale and hence the social coherence of the Palestinians who must be sinking every year deeper into despair as the Israeli occupation persists with no sign of termination.

There is of course a great deal more to Britain's legacy than the sombre tragedy of Palestine. The whole geopolitical configuration of the Eastern Arab world today is to a great extent a derivative of British power and influence. The Ottoman Empire was doomed, like all empires, to eventual decline and fall – we should not forget that it lasted for nearly five hundred years – but it is a fact that, had it not been for Britain, the present successor states, the members of the Arab League, would be far fewer in number than they are. Take the small states of the Persian Gulf, now numbering five from Kuwait to Oman. Without British protection from the early nineteenth century until 1971, these states would unquestionably have been absorbed by Wahhabi, Turkish, Iranian or Egyptian expansionism at some time between 1800 and 1914. Thereafter the British presence, particularly in the 1950s and 1960s, controversial as it was in terms of the power struggles in the Arab world, shielded the small states against the waves of pan-Arabism on the one hand and territorial claims by more powerful neighbours on the other. Furthermore, not only did Britain sustain the integrity of these states, but she also enabled the style of government, and indeed the rule of individual shaikhly families, to persist until the time came for the termination of outside protection.

By the same token, Egypt, which conquered the Sudan in the 1820s, would almost certainly have permanently annexed that country had Britain not become involved during the last twenty years of the nineteenth century, a move which led to the Anglo-Egyptian condominium and, after the Second World War, to Sudanese independence following British resistance to Egyptian monarchist and republican policies aimed at the 'unity of the Nile valley'.

Moreover, the post-1918 carve-up between Britain and France of the Levant Arab provinces led directly to the creation of the modern states of Iraq and Transjordan (now Jordan), a division of five Ottoman governorates (Syria, Mosul, Kirkuk, Baghdad and Basra) which, in other circumstances, might well have secured independence in a quite different pattern.

It is certainly not my intention to seek from those directly concerned praise or gratitude for the part played by Britain in these evolutions, any more than I as an Englishman seek to evade responsibility for Britain's part in the fiasco of Palestine. Britain's role throughout was self-interest and her conduct in certain respects less than honourable. We protected the Persian Gulf states out of regard for the security of communications with the Indian Empire and latterly to protect our oil supplies. We intervened in Egypt and the Sudan also for reasons connected with India. In the Levant we made promises to the Arabs in 1915 which bore no relationship to the eventual outcome arising out of the Peace Settlement of the early 1920s. Because of the importance of our alliance with France, we failed to establish the Arab Kingdom which the Sharifian leaders of the Arab Revolt and their urbanised supporters in Damascus and Baghdad envisaged. We did nothing to prevent France from expelling King Faisal I from Damascus. As a result of this move and the establishment of France's Mandate over Syria, Britain engineered the enthronement of King Faisal in Baghdad and the creation (from the original concept of the Palestine Mandate) of the artificial state of Transjordan under his brother, the Amir Abdullah. Hardly a coherent or an edifying performance. And yet, these creations have taken root and matured into significant sovereign states, members of the Arab League and the United Nations.

Do any traces of British influence remain today in the institutions of these states? Their political systems owe little or nothing to the Westminster model. The amirates of the Gulf are still ruled in the traditional, patriarchal, Arab way originating in the mists of Arab tribal history. The Iraqi version of British-style constitutional monarchy, with the power of the monarch approximating more closely to that of Queen Elizabeth I than Queen Elizabeth II and the parliament structure resembling that of eighteenth-century rather than twentieth-century Britain, was swept away by Brigadier Abdul Karim Qasim in 1958: the rule of Saddam Hussein's Ba'ath Party in 1985 evokes comparison with Eastern Europe, not the United Kingdom. In Egypt, President de Gaulle would find himself on more familiar ground than, say, Mrs Thatcher, in contemplating the political system. The Sudan of ex-President Numeiri and his provisional successors is a far cry from the classical British model which we bequeathed on the independence of the Sudan in 1956. As with the Gulf, we never made a serious attempt, perhaps fortunately, to impose our method of government on the Hashemite Kings of Jordan: King Abdullah and his successor were allowed to go their own idiosyncratic but effective way.

Outside the world of politics, traces of 'Britishness' are perhaps less elusive. Education is an interesting example. Unlike, for instance, France and Spain, it was not the British way, particularly in our imperial heyday, to attempt to export our civilisation and culture to the countries which we controlled. Hence, even though Britain was for so long the paramount power in the Arab world, the great universities in Beirut which contributed so much to the intellectual development and indeed to the growth of Arab nationalism were products not of Oxford or Cambridge but of American missionaries and French priests. Britain ruled Egypt for over half a century but a visitor to Cairo today, if asked which foreign country had exerted the most influence on Egyptian culture in modern times, would almost certainly reply that it must have been France, or perhaps the United States. Of course we introduced the English language throughout the area but this was done for practical reasons, not as part of a 'civilising mission'. It is a sad comment that we founded no universities in the Gulf, in Jordan, in Palestine or even in the Sudan. We controlled education in all these countries for long periods but never reached further than the secondary level. In Lord Kitchener's words, Gordon College (now the University of Khartoum) was designed to produce 'junior native clerks in government service'. The British approach to education in Egypt was on similar lines and I remember my surprise on finding that Baghdad, the former capital of the Abbasid Empire and a major centre of British influence, boasted only a Higher Teachers Training College as recently as 1952. There was no university in Jordan when I served there in the late 1950s and it was only after our decision (in 1968) to terminate our protective treaties with the Gulf states that we helped to found a Technical College in Bahrain to serve the whole Gulf.

Even so, Britain laid the foundation for the spread of the English language throughout the Arab world. Admittedly, it is largely the powerful magnetism of the United States of America which has established English as the second language of all Arabs, but there is far more demand today for higher education, both general and specialised, based in Britain, than there was in our hour of glory. Britain and Iraq, for example, may not share much political common ground, but I believe it to be the case that there are more Iraqi students in the United Kingdom at any one time than there are from any other country in the world, with only one or two exceptions from the Commonwealth. At the University of Exeter where I now work there are over ninety Arab post-graduate students working for masterships and doctorates. We may not have been assiduous in sowing cultural seeds when the field was open to us, but we seem to be reaping a good harvest.

Why does Britain, after years of 'imperialism' followed by rapid decline in power and importance, still exercise attraction for Arabs? Why is the number of Arabs studying in and visiting Britain, or just living here, so much greater in relative, maybe in absolute, numbers than in the United States or elsewhere in Europe? In terms of history, they have good reason to dislike us: military interventions, administrative control, not to speak of the Palestine problem, can scarcely be regarded as sources of popularity, let alone affection.

I think the answer is that, as people, we have a great deal in common, as I have suggested in the earlier chapters of this book. We are both easy-going, humorous, even cosy: perhaps Arabs still feel more at home in such an atmosphere than they do in the more exacting social climates of America or continental Europe. Some years ago the Egyptian nationalist Salama Musa wrote in his memoir *The Education of Salama Musa*: 'I am afraid that, having related the misfortunes which the British imperialists have inflicted on our people, the reader may think that I hate the British – or what I have told him may lead him to hate the British people. I must emphasise my opinion, that they are indeed one of the most noble nations on earth. What I myself enjoy of personal culture and lofty humanitarian values I owe for the better part to the British. I hate only their imperialists ...' And another Arab, Edward Atiyah, wrote in his autobiography, *An Arab Tells His Story*: 'I had often heard Syrians say ... if you want to know the English people as they are by nature, go to their country. There they are genial, hospitable, kind to foreigners. It is only when they come out here as rulers that they become intolerable.'

And of course not all the 'imperialists' were as intolerable as these two authors (and many others) suggest. Arabs are more interested in personalities than in institutions and there have been many Englishmen over the years who are still remembered with love and gratitude, or if not with these particular emotions, at least with respect. What we have bequeathed to the Arab world in terms of military organisation and civil administration, is by far more the legacy of a handful of individuals who have won the confidence of their counterparts than of any systematic governmentally planned policy of 'transfer of technology'.

Maybe it is the case that, the smaller the country, the more lasting the impact of such individuals. It is certainly true that a large number of Englishmen in Egypt over more than half a century, and a relatively large number in Iraq over thirty years, seem to have left little or nothing discernible in today's Egypt or today's Iraq. You have only to read, for example, the works of Lord Cromer, Miss Ger-

trude Bell or, in a lighter vein, those of Major Jarvis and
Lord Edward Cecil to see how hard the British worked in
these two countries and how absolute was their power and
influence at the time. And yet, so little remains of all those
endeavours, at least on the surface. Perhaps mutual respect
was lacking – Lord Edward Cecil's *Leisure of an Egyptian
Official* is still hilariously funny but it makes painful reading
in this particular context; perhaps the indigenous cultures,
particularly in Egypt, ran too deep for another transient
conqueror to achieve anything durable; perhaps the radical
political changes which followed the departure of the
British have obliterated our footprints. By contrast the
punctual, uncomplicated and meritorious public administrative structure of Bahrain in the 1980s represents a demonstrable elaboration of the system inaugurated by Sir
Charles Belgrave, while the recognisably British style and
ethos of the Jordanian military and civil services can be
traced back to the lifetime service of Sir John Glubb and
his fellow officers and of Sir Alec Kirkbride. Reading the
memoirs of these men leaves a profoundly different impression of their relationship with and attitude towards their
Arab colleagues from that of the British officers and officials
of the Egyptian government.

The Sudan falls into a different category. Britain ruled
the country directly for nearly sixty years with the usual
panoply of Governors, Provincial Governors, District Com-
missioners, judges and so on. The Sudan had its own Political and Civil Service recruited on the Indian model. In
brief, British rule in the Sudan was shaped in the straight-
forward colonial model, far removed from the 'veiled protectorates' which we operated elsewhere in the Arab world.
Hence the British tradition, use of the English language and
British attitudes struck deeper roots. Khartoum itself still
has the flavour of a garrison town laid out on geometrical-
lines radiating from the President's (Governor's) Palace.
Omdurman is still the teeming 'native city' across the
river, reminiscent of the distinction between the 'canton-
ment area' and the 'bazaar' of, say, Peshawur. Educated
Sudanese, even of the younger generation, are still
probably more at home in England and with British people

- and vice versa - than is the case with those who did not experience Britain at first hand (the same can be said, curiously, of Palestinians). Lacking wealth (as in the Eastern world) or an exponential increase in population (as in Egypt) physical changes in the towns and cities, in communications and public works, are less glaring than elsewhere.

Which brings me to the British legacy in regard to the broad field of economic and social development. Here again the picture varies enormously between each of the five Arab countries in which I served. Here again individuals, rather than governments, British firms rather than Overseas Aid, have left the deeper marks. As I said earlier, it was never part of British imperial policy to inject finance into overseas territories. The notion of aid to British colonies originated as late as 1945. The colonies were expected to be economically self-supporting. If they had natural resources or other economic advantages they could become rich: if not they remained poor.

The Arab world, with the exception of Jordan which needed British budgetary subsidies for many years in order to survive, was no exception to this policy. In Bahrain, in Iraq, in Jordan the modern infrastructure, industries and services are the products of the Arab oil wealth of the 1960s and 1970s: Egypt is today a beneficiary of oil and of American aid. The Sudan is still poor. But Britain laid many of the foundations - the Gezira Cotton Scheme in the Sudan, major irrigation works in Egypt, the exploitation of Iraqi oil and deep involvement in the early years of the Iraqi Development Board. Lord Cromer may be a leading figure in the demonology of Egyptian nationalism, but even his sternest critics would not deny him credit for his efforts on behalf of the agricultural population. Less famous British experts have left their mark. I think of Jack Eyre of the Middle East Development Division who stage-managed the re-establishment of small businesses and small industries on the stricken West Bank after the first Arab/Israeli war of 1948-9. I think of Sir Edington Miller of the Iraq Development Board, which created the dams and flood control schemes which helped to transform the economy of Iraq in the years before the advent of massive oil wealth. I think of the British consulting engineers and contractors whose achievements still stand, of the British oil companies, the bankers and traders who have all contributed, albeit for their own profit, to the transmutation of an agricultural and bazaar economy to that of the modern, developed world.

I remember, over twenty-five years ago, sitting on a beach outside Beirut with an old and distinguished Englishman, now dead. In a pause in the conversation he said, 'Do you know, today I celebrated my fortieth anniversary of continuous service in the Arab world.' I made what seemed to me the only possible comment: 'You must have seen great changes.' His reply: 'No, none whatsoever!' I saw what he meant at the time. I have now celebrated an even longer, though not continuous, period of association. But I could not answer the same question in the same way, certainly not in regard to the intricate and complex texture of relationships between Britain and the Arabs. The old generation of long-service British 'Middle East hands' has disappeared, whether they were military or civilian officials, teachers, experts, traders, bankers and the rest. The 'Arabist' tradition is now kept alive mainly in the Diplomatic Service, although our Middle-East-based school of Arab studies died with the Lebanese civil war of the 1970s. In their place, paradoxically enough, are far greater numbers of British people living and working in the Arab world than at any time in history – except for the years of the two world wars. Different people in different circumstances, they are engaged in many areas of commerce and industry, many of them the employees of Arab enterprises, generally on short-term engagements, refugees from European unemployment or on stepping-stones to higher things back in Britain. Quite another world altogether from the one I knew.

And, in the other direction, as I have suggested in the case of students, there must be tens of thousands more Arabs in Britain than at any time in the decades up to 1970. I remember, in the early 1950s, escorting a party from a Gulf shaikhdom around London. I recall their bewilderment and sense of unfamiliarity with everything they experienced. Now Britain, particularly after the collapse of the Lebanon, has become a kind of second home to Arabs – studying, visiting, on holiday, on business: it is not long since Arab dress was associated in British minds only with Hollywood, wartime experience, or T. E. Lawrence: now it excites no comment even in small provincial towns. For the last fifteen years a Kuwaiti merchant has been the squire of the small country village in which my old godmother has lived most of her life. I wonder what Lord Cromer or Lord Kitchener would have thought of that.

With this ease of commerce, this coming and going of great numbers in both directions, with the transformation of Britain's place in the world over the past twenty years, the old prejudices – on both sides – arising out of an unequal relationship are, I believe, fast disappearing. When I travel in the Arab world and talk to my Arab friends and acquaintances in Britain, I find that the tendency to see the hidden hand of Britain behind every event, including American policy, in the Middle East has almost vanished, except in jest. The same is most emphatically not true of Iran: even now, six years after the Revolution, the vast majority of Iranian exiles are busy constructing elaborate arguments to support the a priori assumption that the British were the authors of the Shah's downfall and the power behind Ayatollah Khomeini: the Arabs, unless all my interlocutors are being uncharacteristically discreet, seem to have discarded the inferiority complex which breeds this particular variety of piffle. Arabs now are disposed to accept us as we are and their ability to do so is enhanced by their long familiarity with Britain: they understand us as people, they understand our political processes, our institutions, our way of life.

Conversely Britain's century-old experience of the Arab world helps to create a similar understanding, now that the patronising exclusiveness of the imperial officials and the romantic absurdities of the nightshirt-wearing, camel-riding British disciples of T. E. Lawrence have faded into the background of history. Admittedly the old stereotypes of the Arabs as wayward children or hawk-eyed men of the desert, complicated by half-educated and untrustworthy 'effendis', have given way to modern stereotypes of fabulously rich oil shaikhs and murderous Palestinian 'terrorists'. But even these caricatures are, I think, starting to lose conviction. There is no question that the British public media – as distinct from their American counterparts – now present a more rational and less exotic picture of the Arab world than has ever been the case hitherto. At popular level the rapidly growing element of the population which knows the Arab world at first hand is impervious to the old or the new caricatures. The numerous Arab students and their families at the University of Exeter, where I work, appear to fit easily and without discrimination into Devon society, while the many young west country men and women who I have met in trains and shops and who have worked in the Arab world (I could not have written that phrase without exciting incredulity twenty years ago) have a clear, interested and unprejudiced view of the countries in which they have lived. In brief, our understanding, no longer the province of a handful of specialists, has grown too.

All this should form the basis for the best of relations between peoples – knowledge and understanding of each other across the broad field of culture and civilisation, vigorous trade and two-way investment and the interment of the controversies of history. It is thus all the more regrettable that the deep shadow of Palestine continues to darken the horizon. Of course we shall continue to have problems with individual Arab states. What bilateral relationship is free from problems except where there are no worthwhile interests involved? But, until this shadow is lifted by the achievement of a peaceful settlement in which all parties acquiesce, it will continue to cast its cloud.

I have often wondered what my life would have been like if chance had not selected for me a career spent mainly in the Middle East. An idle speculation. All I can say is this. If life consists of ceaseless warfare against boredom, I have been victorious. My wife and I have experienced many excitements, many difficult situations, periodical discomfort and occasional alarums and excursions over the past thirty-five years. But it has always been interesting, absorbingly so, and we have made many good and lasting friends

161

along the way. Our children have grown up in the climate of an ancient civilisation and have become steeped in the fortunes of the modern Middle East: one of them may even follow in an approximation of my own footsteps. We have no regrets.

Index

Abadan oil refinery, 2, 5, 104
Abboud, General Ibrahim, 82, 91, 94, 97, 101
Abdulillah, Prince Regent of Iraq, 6, 17, 20, 22
Abdullah, King of Jordan, 41, 50, 154
Abu Dhabi, 105, 121, 122, 132
Aden, 4, 108, 125, 145
Ajman, 121
Alexandria, 51–2, 68, 69
Amer, Field-Marshal Abdul Hakim, 72
Amin, Sayyid, 112
Amman, 33, 36, 46, 47
Anglo-Iranian Oil Company, 2, 5, 7
Ankara, 33, 53
Aqaba, Jordan, 36
Arabian Gulf *see* Gulf States
Arab-Israeli wars, 148; (1948) 11, 13, 37; (1956) 34; (1967) 45, 46, 48, 75–6, 127–31
Arab League, 6, 44, 45, 145, 153
Arab Revolt (1916), 6, 7, 37, 49–50, 153
Arafat, Yasser, 76
Arthur, Geoffrey, 57, 68
Ass, the (Siamese cat), 79–81, 89, 109
Aswan High Dam, 35, 65, 75, 89
Atiyah, Edward, 156

Babylon, 28–9
Baghdad: British Embassy, 8, 18–19, 28; clubs, 21, 27; daily life in, 21–4, 27; modern, 26–8;

riots, 18–19, 49; train journey to, 5–6
Baghdad Pact, 34
Bahrain, 4, 100, 114; Britain, relations with, 115, 118–19, 126, 128–31; British presence in, 105, 117, 119–20, 132–5, 143, 145; communications, 141–2; contemporary, 140–6; courts, 110; defence, 118, 119, 125, 132, 135, 136, 146; economy, 114–15, 115–16, 125, 126, 135, 136, 138–9, 142–3, 145; education, 114, 155; future alliances, 121–2, 135, 145; government structure, 115, 117–18, 144; independence, 132–5, 136, 140, 145; industry, 115–16, 119, 126, 135, 142, 143; and Iran, 105, 116, 122, 135–7, 139–40, 145; liquor laws, 110; oil, gas, 104, 115, 126, 142; and Palestine, 127–31; regime, 106, 115, 116–17, 138, 144; sects, 114–15; slaves, manumission, 111; social life, 120, 122–5, 137–9; stability, 116–17, 125–6, 131, 144
Bahrain Petroleum Company, 126
Balfour Declaration (1917), 148
Bandoeng Conference (1955), 59
Basra, Iraq, 3
Beeley, Sir Harold, 71
Belgian Congo, 63–4
Belgrave, Sir Charles, 117, 157
Bell, Gertrude, 7, 156–7
bird-watching, 123–4
Boyce, Brigadier Arthur, 10

163